Income
and Health

Allison Quick and
Richard G Wilkinson

Published by the Socialist Health
Association

Authors' Acknowledgement

A number of people gave us valuable help during the preparation of this report. They include Christine Hogg, Mark Minford, Carey Oppenheim, Phyllis Quick, Rosemary Ross, Joyce Rosser, Alex Scott-Samuel, Jenny Shaw and Dick Watson.

Publishers' Acknowledgements

The research for **Income and Health** was funded by the Webb Trust. Research and development for this series **Towards Equality in Health** was generously supported by the Lord Ashdown Trust, through Ruskin College. The Webb Trust has kindly contributed to the printing and publication costs of the series.

Income and Health, by Allison Quick and Richard G Wilkinson
First published by Socialist Health Association
195 Walworth Road, London SE17 1RP

ISBN 0 900687 17 7
Any views expressed in this book are not necessarily those of the Socialist Health Association.

Designed and printed by RAP Limited
201 Spotland Road, Rochdale, Lancs, OL12 7AF

Contents

Introduction

The key argument of this report can be stated in three sentences. **Overall health standards in developed countries are highly dependent on how equal or unequal people's incomes are. The most effective way of improving health is to make incomes more equal. This is more important than providing better public services or making everyone better off while ignoring the inequalities between them.**

The aim of this report is to bring the results of some recent academic research to a wider readership, and to consider its policy implications. This may sound remote from the worries of many of those concerned with public health. But in fact it deals with one of the most exciting new perspectives on the determinants of health which has come to light for many years. It provides an opportunity to gain rapid advances in overall health standards while simultaneously making major reductions in the health disadvantage of the less well-off.

This may seem to be simply a reflection of the familiar concern with material conditions among the relatively poor. But it is much more than that. Essentially, there is something about the quality of life in an unequal society that is damaging to people's health, over and above the direct effects of the material conditions themselves. The health benefits of income redistribution to the population as a whole are much too great to be explained by a reduction in the health disadvantage of the poor alone. This is a crucial point.

It is widely accepted that the main problem of poverty in Britain and other developed societies is relative rather than absolute poverty. Increasingly discussions of the amount of money people need to live on to avoid poverty focus less on minimum material standards than on the idea of a minimum needed to be part of the mainstream of society, to take part in the activities and share the aspirations of society as a whole and to maintain one's self-esteem. But in relation to health, discussions of the effects of poverty still tend to focus exclusively on the material deprivation it causes. There is a steady stream of otherwise excellent reports focusing on matters such as the prevalence of damp housing among the poor, the deterrent effect of charges for health services on take-up, and on the difficulty of shopping for a healthy diet on social security benefits. Such issues have been the traditional focus of those concerned with inequality in health.

Yet the evidence points clearly to the fact that differences in material conditions are not in themselves the most important factor in determining health. This point is argued in more detail later, but understanding it is so fundamental that it is worth outlining just two reasons why the main health effects of income differences cannot be regarded as the result of simple material processes. First, that the average standard of living may be twice as high in some developed countries as in others without any benefit to health, shows that absolute material standards are no longer crucial. Although the poor in the richest countries tend to have higher standards of consumption than the poor in the poorer developed countries, it seems to have little effect on their health. However, what does make a dramatic difference is how much poorer they are relative to other people in their society. It is relative rather than absolute income that counts. The second point is that the benefits of income redistribution are too large and spread too widely across the majority of the population for them to be the results of changes in material deprivation among a poor minority alone. It appears that health standards improve most rapidly as income differences throughout the population get smaller. Economic inequality probably has its main effect on health through psychological and social processes such as the damage it does to people's self-confidence, to social relations and to the quality of the social fabric.

To take these results on board requires a reorientation of much of the thinking which has shaped even the more radical traditions of the public health movement. We have frequently found people responding to the evidence with apparent understanding and growing excitement only to confound us by coming up with comments which show that its real implications have been missed. 'But there is no point in throwing money at people if public services are still lousy' or 'more money won't make any difference unless people are encouraged to spend it sensibly.' (Even on its own, income transferred from the rich to the poor seems to make a lot of difference.) Another common response is 'You seem to think that money is the only thing that matters'. (No, but we are impressed by the evidence that income differences have such a profound impact on things like social relations and people's sense of self-worth which matter very much.)

The idea that public health depends primarily on better public services is a fallacy. Services such as better housing, public transport, clean, well-lit streets, home helps, a well funded NHS are vital to the quality of people's lives. They should be a priority for government spending. They will undoubtedly have an effect on health — perhaps by more numerous routes than are usually recognised. But purely from the health point of view the need for better public services should not be allowed to divert attention from the even greater need for income redistribution. In particular, improvements in health should not be seen as dependent on 'getting the economy right' so that more can be spent on public services. Health need not wait for what the Labour Party has started to call 'the growth dividend'. There are poorer countries with better health and richer countries with worse. Indeed it is salutary to note that it was during the two World Wars, when resources and material infrastructure of society was most overstretched, that civilian life expectancy in Britain achieved its most rapid increases. For Britain to become an even more wealthy society is neither a necessary nor a sufficient condition for more rapid advances in health. But, given current levels of affluence, becoming a more equal society is both a necessary and a sufficient condition.

Reducing economic inequality has to be the main public health task for the immediate future. Despite the concern over poverty, those involved in public health have not, in general, devoted their professional attention to how this should be done. Inequality of incomes is a function both of the differences in original incomes and of the way that is adjusted by the tax and benefit system. What comes as a surprise to some is that differences in taxes and benefits account for a large part of the differences in the amount of inequality in the developed countries. For better or worse, whether they like it or not, governments exercise a very substantial measure of control over what is probably the most important determinant of health in the developed world. We therefore make no apology for devoting a considerable part of this report to explaining the major issues involved in reforming the tax/benefit system. It is essential that public health advocates and all those who are concerned with the population's health gain a better understanding of what is involved in making the tax/benefit system more redistributive.

However, there are few subjects that are more complicated or controversial. We have avoided technicalities as much as possible and have dealt only briefly with short-term policies (such as the need to link pensions to wage inflation or the advantages of increasing child benefit). These matters have been thoroughly covered elsewhere. Instead, the discussion in the latter part of this report focuses on the issues of principle involved in making more fundamental reforms. It is hoped that the discussion will help to familiarise people with the issues that should be at the centre of debates over public health policy.

The three sections which follow this introduction discuss the evidence on the relationship between income and health. Sections 4, 5, 6 and the Endnote deal with the implications of this evidence for policy and outline the issues involved in making the tax and benefit system fundamentally more redistributive.

1

Income and health: the evidence

It is widely recognised that poverty and ill-health go hand in hand. But despite this, the crucial relationship between income and health is usually misunderstood. Two misconceptions are common. The first, based on the experience of the last few generations, is the assumption that rising prosperity remains the main source of improved standards of health throughout society. As standards of comfort improve so, it is thought, will health. The second misconception is that the only remaining relationship between income and health is the residual relationship between absolute poverty and ill-health. It is assumed that such a relationship will weaken and then disappear as affluence spreads further down the social scale sweeping the last remnants of 'real' need before it. Once everyone has attained certain minimum material standards, has a dry house large enough for the family, can afford to heat it, is able to buy adequate food and clothing with a little money in hand for emergencies and extras, that will be the end of any causal relationship between income and health.

A closer look at the evidence shows that both these views are wrong. Economic growth no longer ensures rising standards of health, and the elimination of absolute poverty will not neutralise the important influence which income has on health. The health problems of modern societies follow a new pattern which places the social structure under a much more critical light. The picture emerging from recent research is a startling one. Once societies have reached the levels of affluence found in the developed countries, further improvements in **absolute** standards make rather little difference to health. Health differences between developed countries reflect, not differences in wealth, but differences in income distribution, in the degree of income inequality, within each society. Among the developed countries this seems to be the single most important determinant of why health in one country is better than in another.

Although income differentials and **relative** poverty have a profound effect on the scale of health inequalities within each society, we are not concerned here simply with health **inequalities**. Income distribution is one of the key determinants of health standards across society as a whole. This has important policy implications: it suggests that we do not face a choice between maximising overall health status or reducing health inequalities. Quite the reverse. The message is not simply that inequality kills the poorest, but that it reaches well beyond the poor to become the major determinant of health standards among the population as a whole. The evidence leaves little room to doubt that a major programme of income redistribution is now an essential part of an effective policy for public health.

Most of the research mentioned in the following pages is recent and the picture it provides of the relationship between income and health is not well known even to many people working in community medicine and public health. We shall therefore go through the evidence carefully.

International comparisons

In order to distinguish the wood from the trees we shall, before looking at the relationship between health and income among individuals, start by noting some important relationship to be found in the international data.

Among the less developed countries there is still a clear relationship between their average per capita income and measures of health such as average life expectancy. The higher the standard of living in these countries, the healthier they are. Although the relationship is not perfect, it is statistically strong and highly significant.[1] However, among the much richer industrial — or post-industrial — countries, improvements in health are no longer strongly related to rates of economic development and increasing per capita incomes (see figure 1).

Figure 1: The lack of relationship between GNP per capita and average life expectancy in rich countries. Each point represents a country.

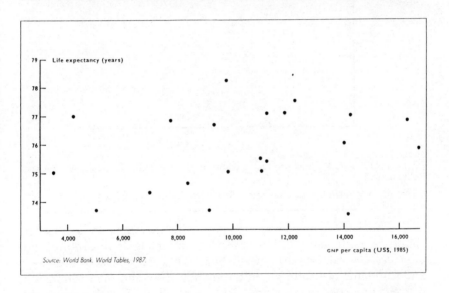

Source: World Bank. World Tables, 1987.

Figure 1 represents a group of rich countries on their own. What happens to the overall relationship across both rich and poor countries is shown in Figure 2.

Figure 2 shows that health is only strongly related to the standard of living among countries below a threshold level of income. Above about $5,000 (1985) per capita the health curve levels out and, as economists would say, further increases in income lead to diminishing health returns (figure 2).

Figure 2: The relationship between GNP per capita and life expectancy in rich and poor countries.

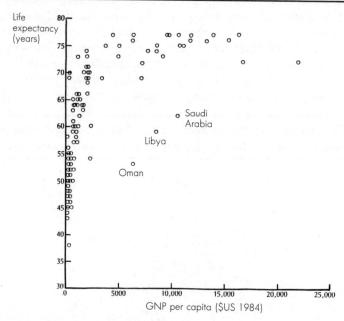

GNP per capita ($US 1984)

(The rich Middle Eastern oil-producing countries with low life expectancy are marked individually.)

(Reproduced with kind permission from C Marsh, **Exploring Data**, p213, Polity Press, 1988)

We shall concentrate here on what happens in the richer countries, particularly Britain. Clearly economic growth continues to raise levels of real income in these countries (except in years of recession) and standards of health go on improving. However, the relationship between these two trends is very weak. Not only are growth rates poorly related to the rate of improvement in health, but health in some of the richer countries, like the United States, Luxembourg or (what was) West Germany, is worse than in poorer countries such as Spain and Greece with considerably lower average incomes.

However, among the developed countries there is a striking relationship between the **distribution** of income and health. As figure 3 shows, there is a clear tendency for people in the countries with the fairest distribution of income to have the longest life expectancy. This relationship exists among both rich and poor countries.[2] But as increases in the average level of income or absolute standard of living become less and less important among the richer countries, income distribution becomes more and more important.

Figure 3: The relationship between income distribution and life expectancy.

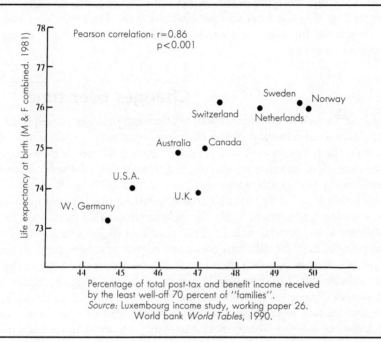

Percentage of total post-tax and benefit income received
by the least well-off 70 percent of "families".
Source: Luxembourg income study, working paper 26.
World bank *World Tables*, 1990.

The evidence of the importance of income distribution does not hang on the evidence of figure 3 alone. Indeed, the basic cross-sectional relationship has now been demonstrated four times using different measures of income distribution from different countries at different dates.[2,3,4,5] As well as being robust, it is, statistically speaking, a very strong relationship. Despite the small number of countries for which comparable data was available for figure 3, the correlation is highly significant and suggests that about two-thirds of the variation in life expectancy between these countries is related to differences in their income distributions.

The fact that the relationship between income distribution and life expectancy (or death rates) cannot be dismissed as a statistical artifact does not prove that it is causal. It may, for instance, be thought that

13

it is a reflection of a tendency for more egalitarian societies to have better public services which could benefit health. Differences in the provision of medical services are however unlikely to be the explanation. Modern medical care has surprisingly little influence on mortality in developed countries, and using statistical methods to control for any effect of differences in the level of public and private expenditure on medical care does not alter the relationship with income distribution.[5] Not only is it hard to think of other possibilities of this kind which are worth investigating, but there is a variety of other evidence which strongly suggests causality.

Changes over time

As well as an international relationship between life expectancy and income distribution observed cross-sectionally at various points in time, there is also evidence that the two are related as they change over time. The fact that equally strong relationships between income distribution and death rates have been found at different dates is in itself enough to imply that any changes during the intervening years were at least consistent with the relationship. This has now been confirmed in several ways.[6] The problem is of course to find comparable data for different countries at two or more points in time to allow changes between those points to be analysed. A small set of very reliable data for a few OECD countries showed a highly significant relationship between the annual rate of change of life expectancy and the annual rate of change of income distribution over different time periods. As income distribution narrowed, life expectancy increased more rapidly. This time-series correlation was as close as in the cross-sectional data shown in figure 3. Despite using much less comparable data from World Bank sources, a statistically significant but weaker relationship was also found for a larger group of countries.

More intuitively appealing evidence comes from the contrast between the experience of Britain and Japan. At the beginning of the 1970s income distribution and life expectancy were quite similar in the two countries: on both counts they were close to the average of the OECD countries for which data was available. Since then Japan has become a very much more egalitarian society. It now has the most egalitarian income distribution in the world and, at the same time, has achieved the longest life expectancy in the world.[7] Britain on the other hand has become much less egalitarian. The gap between rich and poor widened dramatically during the 1980s and differences in earnings reached their widest for over a century. Movements in death rates reflect this deterioration: since 1985 British death rates for men and women aged 16-45 years have actually been increasing — even after excluding AIDS deaths.[8] Such dramatic examples strongly suggest that changes in income distribution and life expectancy are causally related. Indeed, even the annual rate of change of death rates in Britain seems to be related to the degree of income inequality in the country.[6]

Within Britain the periods which have seen the most rapid increases in life expectancy also stand out as periods of particularly rapid income redistribution. Paradoxically, during the two World Wars civilian life expectancy increased two or three times as fast as it did during the rest of the century.[9] This happened despite the war-time disruption of daily life, the worry and stress felt by the families of conscripts, the overstretching of medical services and the deterioration in material circumstances. While the healthier diet which resulted from food rationing is likely to have made a contribution in the Second World War, if could not have done so in the First. What both periods have in common however is that both wars were periods of dramatic income redistribution. As well as seeing the virtual elimination of unemployment and very favourable trends in earnings differentials, both wars saw attempts to ensure at least minimum standards of provision for all. As Titmuss pointed out, the desire for social justice and the attempt to create a more equitable distribution of income and wealth were an important part of the war strategy. *"If the co-operation of the masses was thought to be essential (to the prosecution of war), then inequalities had to be reduced and pyramid of social stratification had to be flattened."*[10] The war-time improvements in health were apparently greatest in areas where health had been worst.[9]

Confirmation that the substantial degree of war-time income redistribution was influential comes from the more accurate data on income distribution available annually for the last few decades. It looks as if even the annual rate of change in death rates in Britain is statistically related to the usually minor upward and downward trends in the degree of income inequality in the country.

It would seem reasonable to suppose that the effect of income redistribution on national standards of health operates by just such a levelling up process. One would expect health differences within the population to diminish as the health of the poorest improved in response to income redistribution.

It is possible to test whether this is happening by seeing if the changes which have taken place in the size of class differences in death rates in Britain reflect trends in the scale of relative poverty. The indications are that they do. Research shows that social class differences in death rates have widened during periods when the proportion of people living in relative poverty has increased, and narrowed when it has deceased.[11] Before, during and immediately after the Second World War differentials in earnings narrowed and major extensions of social insurance and assistance schemes reduced relative poverty. The result was that class differences in death rates narrowed. By the early 1950s, Britain was a more egalitarian society than it had been before or has been since and its mortality differentials reached the smallest on record. Since then relative poverty has grown, decade by decade, at an accelerating rate. So too has the size of the class differences in death rates. The proportion of the population living in relative poverty (relative to average personal disposable income) has increased from about eight percent in the early 1950s to some thirty percent in the early 1980s. Over the same period the difference in death rates between classes has doubled or trebled.[11*]

We have seen that there is evidence of a relationship between income distribution and health across countries at a point in time. We have also seen that this relationship holds for changes over time — whether you look at changes within a period in a number of countries or at changes over a number of periods within one country. Lastly, we have seen that this relationship seems to work, as one would expect, by narrowing mortality differences within the population. We shall now turn to evidence of a relationship between income and health among smaller groups and individuals within the population.

Population sub-groups

If more equal incomes increase average life expectancy, this suggests that changes in relative incomes must make a bigger difference to the health of the poor than to that of the rich. Several bits of rather crude cross-sectional evidence on the relationship between the death rates and incomes of different occupations and social classes in Britain have suggested that this might be so.[13,3] Though not above criticism, that data suggested that mortality rates rise increasingly rapidly as you move down the income scale.

Much sounder and more recent individual data comes from the Health and Lifestyles Survey and is shown in figure 4. This survey of some 7,000 people was carried out in 1984-85 and used three different measures of health covering disability, physical and psychological

Figure 4: Income and Health: age-standardised health ratios, illness and psycho-social health, in relation to weekly income, demonstrating the effect of £50/week increments in household income, males and females age 40-59 (all of a given age and gender = 100).

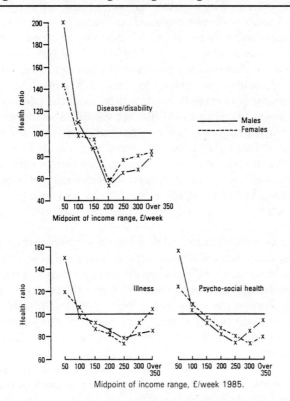

(Reproduced with kind permission from Blaxter, M, **Health and Lifestyle**, London, Tavistock, 1990, p73)

health.[14] The shape of the curves are consistent with very substantial improvements in the health of the poor as income is transferred from the rich to the poor. Not only does the shape of these curves imply that the health of the rich may not suffer but, perhaps rather implausibly, suggests they may even benefit from a reduction in their relative wealth.

The most rigorous method of establishing causality is the randomised controlled trial. As yet, no one has set up such a trial to test the effects of income supplementation on health among the relatively poor in the developed world. There was however a randomised controlled trial designed to study the economic effects of negative income tax among a relatively poor population in Gary, Indiana, in the 1970s. Incomes in the experimental group were substantially increased by negative income tax and, although the effects on general health were not assessed, differences in the incidence of low birthweight babies were. It was found that the increase in incomes consequent on negative income tax significantly reduced the incidence of babies born at dangerously low birthweights to high risk mothers.[15]

The difficulty of trying to establish causality by purely observational methods is that the rich differ from the poor in too many ways to compare like with like. Whether we take a snapshot at a point in time or follow people as they get richer or poorer, the same problem arises. Even if you control for education and social class, it may be suggested that results reflect more amorphous things such as culture, 'initiative' or intelligence. The only way observational methods can avoid selective bias is by studying the effects of changes in income brought about by factors blind to the prior characteristics of the individuals affected.

A study which attempted to avoid these problems looked to see how the mortality rates of whole occupational groups were affected by the changes in occupational earnings differentials during a period which covered both the inflation of the mid 1970s and the industrial upheavals which took place in the few years following 1979.[4] The aim was to see whether occupations which changed their place in the 'earnings league' over a ten year period showed corresponding changes in their place in the mortality league. Instead of taking changes simply in the average earnings in each occupation, the study used data on the proportion of people earning different percentages of the average income for all occupations. It also included data on changes in occupational unemployment. The results showed that changes in occupational mortality rates were strongly related to changes in the proportion of people in each occupation earning less than about sixty percent of the national average. Changes in the proportion of people unemployed in each occupation had a similar, independent, effect. The results suggested that people who became unemployed or moved into the low earnings category suffered a thirty or forty percent increase in their risk of death. The fact that changes in the proportion of people in the middle and upper income groups appeared to have no direct impact on mortality rates lends additional support to the role of income redistribution.

State old-age pensions provide another example of income changes which operate independently of the personal characteristics of the people affected. As more than half of all old-age pensioners live on very small incomes it might be expected that their health would be affected by changes in the real value of pensions. A statistical analysis was undertaken to test for a relationship between the annual changes in the real value of pensions and national death rates of old people.[3] Using the death rates of people below pensionable age as controls, it found a close relationship even after allowing for any influence of changes in GNP per capita. The value of state pensions appears to exert a strong influence on the death rates of old people in Britain.

Several studies have of course shown that the unemployed suffer increased illness and raised death rates as a result of their unemployment. Their poorer health cannot be accounted for in terms of an increased tendency for the sick to become unemployed.[16,17] The excess mortality **each year** among unemployed men and their wives has been estimated to amount to some 1,500 extra deaths per one million men employed.[18] Whether the health effects of unemployment are a consequence of loss of wages or of related factors such as the loss of self-esteem is not clear, but the similar effects of unemployment and low earnings on occupational death rates (above) suggest that loss of income plays a substantial part.

When looking at relationships such as that between income and health it is often suggested that the causal relationship might be the other way round from that described here. Instead of changes in income distribution affecting health, a tendency for sick people to become poorer would mean that poorer health would widen the income distribution. The possibility of so-called 'reverse causality' has been carefully examined in a number of major studies on class and health and on unemployment and health. Although the sick do suffer economically, the direct effects of poverty on sickness seem to be considerably more important. In addition, several of the studies mentioned above — such as the one on the value of state pensions and old people's death rates, studies of unemployment and health, of changing occupational incomes and occupational mortality rates — were specifically designed to avoid the possibility of reverse causation producing misleading results.

Unlike studies of social class and health, which are based on the economically active population in the working age range (from 20 years to retirement), the strongest evidence of the importance of income distribution comes from figures of life expectancy for the total population throughout life. Because these are heavily influenced by deaths in childhood and in later life, when people are not earning, there is less scope for reverse causation. Indeed, it is possible to trace a statistically significant relationship between changes in death rates for children (0-19 years old). Lastly, there is fairly clear evidence that income distribution is determined by economic forces, by the trade cycle and by changes in taxes and benefits, rather than by health.

We have now looked at the relationship between income and health cross-sectionally and in time-series, internationally and nationally, within population subgroups and individuals, and the evidence clearly suggests that income distribution is a major determinant of standards of health across society as a whole.

---

* Instead of simply comparing the death rates of the top and bottom social classes, the change in size of social class differences in death rates is measured across all classes and takes into account the changing class distribution of the population and revisions to the social class classification. See[12]

2 Inequalities in health

Part of the way in which income distribution raises overall standards of health is, as we have seen, by improving the health of the poor and narrowing the health gap. Later, we shall see that this is by no means the whole story: the health benefits of income redistribution are too large to be accounted for in terms of health gains among the poor alone. Although the primary objective should probably be the maximisation of overall standards of health, equity in health is an important and desirable goal in itself. Indeed, the reduction of health inequalities is the first of the World Health Organization's European Targets.[19]

Most of the data on socioeconomic differences in health come from the Registrar General's decennial figures showing differences in death rates between people classified by occupational class. Those figures show that the reduction in life expectancy at birth for people in unskilled occupations amounts to some seven or eight years — a loss of about ten percent of life. At most ages death rates are about twice as high among unskilled manual workers and their families as they are among professional classes. This means that twice as many of a person's circle of friends and contemporaries would die prematurely each year in one class as in the other. When it comes to illness, the differences are of a similar size: twice as many lower as upper class people say they suffer from chronic illnesses that limit their activity.

How many excess deaths result from the higher death rates in lower socioeconomic groups? We can calculate the proportion of deaths among men and women **of working age** which would be prevented if the death rates of all manual social classes were reduced to the level of all non-manual social classes. This produces a figure of some 22,000 excess deaths a year which, because they consist of deaths occurring between the ages of 16 and normal retirement, are all premature deaths. Unfortunately problems of classifying a large proportion of the total population including the old, the young and women who are not employed, means that there is no reliable way of estimating excess deaths at other ages to produce a total associated with socioeconomic disadvantage. But if we assume that socioeconomic disadvantage has the same effect on the death rates of all people at all ages as it does to economically active people of working age, we would expect a total of between 100,000 and 200,000 excess deaths annually. Most of these additional deaths would of course be in later life.

Over the last generation or so these health differences have shown no sign of diminishing. Indeed, the tendency for the health gap to widen even during decades when most people — ignorant of the trends in relative poverty — assumed that Britain was becoming a more egalitarian society, led to doubts about whether the figures could be taken at face value.

For example, it was suggested that people in lower classes had worse health, not because of the circumstances in which they lived, but because people with worse health are more likely to suffer downward social mobility. Instead of being less healthy because they lived in less good conditions, it was suggested that people ended up in less good conditions because they were unhealthy.

Data from a number of large cohort studies (which collect information from a sample of the population over a number of years) have now been used to measure the relationship between health and social mobility. They found that although illness does influence social mobility, this relationship only accounts for a small part of the overall class differences in health.[20,21] Much the larger part of the health disadvantage of lower classes has to be seen as a product of their socioeconomic disadvantage.

A number of other more technical problems of measurement and comparison were also raised but, on investigation, were found not to make much difference to the picture we have (see for instance[12,22]).

Reducing health inequalities

It is almost certainly unrealistic to believe that it is possible to develop policies which would reduce health inequalities without tackling the underlying socioeconomic inequalities. First, the excess deaths are not the result of just one or two preventable diseases. Instead, the vast majority of diseases are more common lower down the social scale. Nor can the imbalance be attributed to the known behavioural influences on health. For example, differences in death rates among diseases unrelated to smoking are just as great as for diseases which are related to smoking.[23] In fact, modern knowledge of the causes of disease is still quite unable to account for most of the class differences. Very little is known about how to prevent many of the important causes of death. Even with a disease such as heart disease, which has been much more thoroughly researched than most, the known risk factors explain a good deal less than half the class differences in death rates.[24]

But even where we do know the risk factors, they are often only partially controllable. Sometimes this is because health advice has only a very minor influence on behaviour, and sometimes it is because even if everyone followed all the do's and don'ts of healthy living to the letter, it would only lead to a minor reduction in the underlying physiological risk. For instance, the amount of fat in the diet is only one of a number of determinants of blood cholesterol levels, and they in turn, are only one of several determinants of heart disease. Even if adults changed their diets enough to lower their blood cholesterol levels by ten percent for forty years, only one in fifty men and one in four hundred women would have prevented a heart attack before their 55th birthday.[25]

Most of the published evaluations of projects which have attempted to influence health related behaviour suggest that health advice has, with a few exceptions, only a minor influence on most people's behaviour.[26] In part this probably reflects people's understandable scepticism about how much difference behaviour change will make to their health. But the frequent and well documented failure of so many health education projects suggests that it is unwise to approach behaviour change as if people's drinking, smoking, exercise and dietary patterns were not bound up with every other aspect of their lives. It is precisely because behaviour **is** related to personal circumstances that the behavioural risk factors so far identified are systematically related to social class.

Finally, it would be wrong to think that health differences result from differences in medical care. First, although differences in medical care exist, they are relatively small in comparison to the differences in health. But even if they were not, medicine is largely ineffective in relation to some of the most important modern causes of death. The fact that the first symptom of heart disease and stroke is often sudden death clearly limits the scope for medical intervention. Among some of the most common cancers the lack of any long-term improvement in case-fatality rates suggests that medical treatment has rather little impact on death rates. Although there are class differences in case-fatality rates for cancers and heart disease, they do not seem to be related to differences in medical care and are anyway overshadowed by the scale of class differences in the incidence of these diseases.[27] The controversy which exists about the influence of medical care on death rates is less about how large it is as about whether it is measurable at all.

It has to be accepted that health inequalities are, first and foremost, a testament to the continued strength of socioeconomic influences on health. Health inequalities could only be reduced while leaving the underlying socioeconomic inequalities intact if known risk factors accounted for more than a small fraction of the overall burden of ill-health and if they could easily be prized from their social context. However, whether or not the aim is considered desirable, the fact that this is not the situation leaves us little choice. Even tackling known risk factors in such a way as to reduce, rather than widen, health inequalities is beset with difficulties. Take smoking for example. It is often said that health education campaigns widen class differentials in smoking and that it would be better to increase the tobacco tax. But it has been calculated that smokers among the poorest twenty percent of households already spend nine percent of their disposable incomes just on tobacco tax.[28] Paying additional tax may well add to the health problems of those who are not deterred from smoking. A realistic policy for reducing inequalities in health must then address itself to the underlying socioeconomic inequalities.

Income almost certainly provides the best means of tackling health inequalities. Income differences come close to the core of the underlying socioeconomic inequalities; they exert a powerful influence on health. Income distribution and levels of relative poverty are highly sensitive to policy on taxes and benefits. Data from the Health and Lifestyles Survey suggests that the association between social class and health is primarily an association between income and health.[14] Although there must be other features of socioeconomic status which affect health, few are as accessible to policy as income.

3 How income affects health

Not only the poor

Although the evidence suggests that making incomes more equal would have its greatest effect on the health of those in relative poverty, it looks as if its impact on health is too great to be explained wholly by health improvements among the poor. In the early 1980s, when income differentials were not as wide as they are now, British life expectancy at birth was around three years shorter than that of Japan and the most egalitarian European societies. About two years of this short-fall seems to be associated with differences in income distribution.

Unfortunately we do not know the life expectancy of the twelve percent of the British population who in 1981 came within the European Community definition of relative poverty (living on less than fifty percent of the average). Social class V, whose death rates we do know, accounted for only about six percent of the economically active population and may therefore represent a more extreme group. However, let us assume that the twelve percent then living in relative poverty had death rates equivalent to those found in social class V. If we then calculate the effect on the population's average life expectancy of bringing those death rates down to the average, we find such a change would account for only about six months of the two-year short fall in British life expectancy. To account for the whole two years it would be necessary to assume that the least well off **quarter** of the population overcame a health disadvantage **twice** as great as that suffered by social class V. Despite using many different measures of socioeconomic disadvantage, no one has yet identified such a large proportion of the population at such a high risk.

If we were nevertheless to assume that all the improvement in life expectancy came from a levelling up process of this kind, it might be expected to lead to the disappearance of existing health inequalities. But the more egalitarian societies like Norway, Sweden and the Netherlands, have not abolished their internal health inequalities. Though apparently smaller than the differences found in Britain, they still have substantial health inequalities.[29] While Japanese income distribution and life expectancy have improved rapidly, health gains have (in contrast to the British experience) been faster among blue-collar than white-collar workers but important differences still remain between them.[7]

Together, these considerations suggest that the health differences between the more and less egalitarian developed countries cannot be attributed wholly to differences in the numbers and health of the relatively poor in each country. The implication is that the health of other sections of the population must also benefit from income redistribution. If you take figures of the proportion of income going to the least well-off ten, twenty, thirty percent and so on in each country, you find that the relationship with life expectancy reaches its strongest when you take the proportion of income going to the bottom sixty or seventy percent of the population. This not only makes sense in terms of the size of the health benefits, but it rather neatly points to average income as the line which separates the gainers from the remainder. Because the distribution of income is skewed by a small number of very rich people who push the average up, a little over sixty percent of the population live on less than the average. (More sophisticated measures of inequality, such as the Gini coefficient, which measure inequality across the whole population are almost equally closely related to life expectancy.)

What are the links?

Greater income equality seems to create a healthier society as a whole. How can this be explained? What sort of factors link health and income distribution? The first thing to remember is that we are dealing primarily — as figure 2 shows — with the effects of relative income and poverty, not with the effects of absolute income levels. It is not how rich or poor people are in absolute terms which matters, but how rich or poor they are in relation to others in their society.

Although some developed countries have per capita incomes three times as high as others there are no consistent differences in health between them. If it was absolute poverty which affected health we would expect health to improve as increasing wealth led to a diminution in absolute poverty. Levels of absolute poverty could only remain untouched by increasing affluence if income differentials tended to widen as countries got richer. However, there is no evidence that they do — rather the reverse.

Large differences in absolute income appear then to have little or no effect on mortality, but small differences in income distribution appear to have a large effect. This provides fairly clear evidence that it is relative standards, or differences, rather than absolute standards which matter.

If the issue is not absolute income levels, this suggests that health is no longer determined primarily by the directly physiological effects of the material circumstances in which people live. The importance of relative income implies that the crucial issue is what a person's income or standard of living means in the social context of their society. The problem lies less in the physical consequences of the material conditions of life than with their psychological and emotional consequences.

An example may clarify the issue. There are still numerous ways in which differences in people's physical circumstances continue to have a direct effect on their health. Housing is a case in point. Research has reliably identified a connection between high rates of some respiratory illnesses and the mould spores to which the occupants of damp housing are exposed.[30] Similarly, people living in poorer housing are less likely to have central heating and so are more likely to use types of heating which carry higher fire risks. There are many other examples of ways in which the least well off are more often exposed to direct physical health risks whose consequences they will suffer regardless of their state of mind. Tackling such factors must remain a high priority for public health policy.

The overwhelming importance of relative income suggests that physical exposure to material hazards such as poor housing are no longer the main determinants of health. Much the largest part of the problem is not the **material** concomitants or consequences of relative deprivation, but the fact of **relative** deprivation itself. This means that we have to address ourselves to the more fundamental but more intangible problems of the psychological and social implications of income differences, of relative poverty and of having to live in conditions which are recognisably sub-standard — regardless of what affluence may have done to the standard.

A study which quite incidentally showed the primacy of the psychological over the material links between health and socioeconomic disadvantage was a study of people made redundant when a factory closed. GPs found that increases in both major and minor illnesses among their patients dated from when redundancies were first announced — before people actually became unemployed.[16]

Having said that, it may be that some of the health effects of relative poverty can be avoided by those few who have to some extent **chosen** a cheaper lifestyle. But for most people it is hard to live on a low income without financial worries and stress, without it cramping your style or limiting your social contacts and confidence, and without a sense of diminishing self-esteem and worthlessness. Clearly, the effects of poverty on monks, political activists, self-sufficiency enthusiasts or committed artists may be very different from the effects on someone who would like nothing better than a well paid job. But in societies where appearances count for so much, few will have the emotional resources or the alternative sources of self-esteem to avoid the demeaning effects of a low income.

There are other effects which are unavoidable. The infrastructure of modern societies is constantly developing to meet the needs of people equipped with average or above average resources. Without the necessary resources to keep up, many daily activities are made increasingly difficult. For instance, not having a washing machine is not much of an inconvenience where everyone goes to a local launderette. But in a society where most people have washing machines and launderettes are rare, the poor may be reduced to washing clothes by hand in a council flat which, though provided with plumbing for a washing machine, may have only an unsuitably small sink. Similarly, where most people have a car, the tendency is to site amenities to suit car owners and then to cut back on public transport.

Unless people can afford to equip themselves with the normal range of consumer goods such as a washing machine, car, telephone, cooker and fridge, ordinary tasks become more time consuming and awkward. So much so, that the poor are increasingly excluded from participating in the ordinary life of society. The problem is inherently a relative one in which standards constantly change: watches became a necessity as time-keeping became more important many years ago. As shopping and home life become geared up to the use of frozen foods, it becomes harder to do without freezers. Similarly, as credit cards and credit-worthiness play an expanding role in a wide variety of financial transactions, their lack becomes inconvenient and stigmatising.

At this level poverty is literally disabling. And, like many forms of disability, poverty is also socially handicapping. People with inadequate incomes constantly find themselves at a social disadvantage and may often be unable to participate in ordinary social activities and maintain ordinary social relations. They may not be able to afford to go out with friends or pay for their children to go on a school trip. The expense of visiting family and friends may lead to less frequent contact. It becomes harder to entertain people or to fulfil some of the obligations that a good friend or relative might be expected to. Neediness and an inability to reciprocate turns relationships into one-sided dependencies which many friendships will not survive. As old friendships break up and the social activities needed to make new ones are out of reach, it is not surprising that surveys show that the poor are socially isolated.[31]

Even though, in terms of income levels, we are dealing with relative rather than absolute poverty, that does not mean that people will always give highest priority to the purchase of so-called 'basic necessities'. Having a drink with friends or buying your children clothes that you are not ashamed for them to be seen in may sometimes seem more important than healthy food or adequate heating. Thus, incomes which are theoretically adequate to pay for 'essentials' may, in practice, not be enough to prevent people suffering some of the physiological effects of absolute poverty. This might explain why small surveys have found that a quarter of all parents on what was then Supplementary Benefit had only one meal a day and that at the end of the week a quarter of all people on unemployment benefit did not have enough money left for food.[32,33] No doubt some of the seven percent of pensioners which a DHSS survey found were malnourished preferred to spend less on food in order to have a television to relieve the endless hours of boredom and isolation.[34] Similarly it is clear that for some teenagers it is more important to extricate themselves from family conflicts than to have a roof over their heads. As human beings, our social needs are often as pressing as our physiological needs, and minimum income levels must recognise this.

The state of mind and levels of stress induced by poverty can be seen most clearly in the results of a study of families in bed-and-breakfast accommodation. Forty four percent of the women said they were unhappy most of the time, forty one percent were tired most of the time, thirty five percent often lost their temper, thirty four percent could not sleep at night, thirty three percent said their children got on top of them and twenty four percent said they burst into tears for no reason.[35] Inadequate cooking facilities meant that many families could not even cook regular meals for themselves.

Although people in bed-and-breakfast accommodation may be only a tiny minority, they and others classified as homeless totalled almost 700,000 in 1989.[36] The experience of coping on inadequate incomes is the lot of millions of other people on whom it must have a similar, if less extreme, psychological impact.

The health effects of some of these aspects of poverty and inequality are only too obvious. To point out that we are a long way away from the sense of happiness and well-being which have been found to be predictive of longevity[37] may risk trivialising the picture. However it is worth emphasising that the health disadvantage of the poor is a double injustice: rather than being 'short and sweet', life is short where its quality is poor. Health is often an indicator of the real quality of human life.

No doubt partly as a result of the lack of friends, lack of social support, additional stress and the undermining of self-esteem, the poor tend to smoke more,[38,39] and the number of heavy drinkers[40] and users of prescribed and unprescribed drugs among them may also increase.[41]

Social relations

The key element in understanding the health effects not only of poverty but also of income differentials more generally is likely to be the combination of stress, insecurity and poor social relations. Factors such as stress, 'social support', 'confiding relationships', social participation and self-esteem have all been shown to be closely related to health.[42,43,44] Indeed, good social support is almost certainly protective against some of the health effects of stress, so people who have more stress and less social support are particularly vulnerable.[45,43] The epidemiological evidence suggests that the whole range of social relations have an influence on health — from the most personal domestic relations to people's participation in local community activities — including social relations in the workplace. At the most personal level, surveys have found that women in lower classes are less likely to have the benefit of 'confiding relationships'.[44] No doubt disputes over money, which are a common source of stress and marital conflict, contribute to this pattern. At other levels, a study of some 17,000 office-based civil servants found that the most senior staff were not only more likely than junior staff to see a confidante daily, but were also much more likely to have social contact with neighbours and with people from work.[23]

While psycho-social problems of stress, self-esteem and social relations are most severe among the poor, their effects will be felt with diminishing frequency all the way up the social scale. If the health disadvantage of the least well off is mainly a problem of relative position, of expectations and standards informed — as they must be — by comparison with others, then it is easy to see why the health effects of income distribution are not confined to the poor. A sense of relative deprivation can exist in varying degrees over most of the income range — from the poorest right up to within striking distance of the richest. Large income differentials have always been regarded as socially divisive: and close friendships are difficult between people with very different resources at their disposal. It is likely that income differentials affect levels of stress, insecurity and the quality of social relations throughout society so that the more divided a society is, the more strain it is likely to place on individuals within it.

One might speculate that the war-time improvements in civilian life expectancy were partly a product of the sense of camaraderie and shared purpose which older people so frequently recall. Indeed, as well as an improved income distribution giving rise to better social relations, the sense of a common bond probably also facilitated the development of war-time policies intended to ensure minimum standards of provision for all. It is hard to know here which caused which, and there are clearly possibilities for the development of virtuous — or, conversely, vicious — circles in this field. No doubt the growing sense of social cohesion during the war was an important factor contributing to the election of the 1945 Labour government committed to the expansion of the welfare state.

Societies with wide income differentials and inadequate anti-poverty policies, with high rates of homelessness and unemployment, might be expected to suffer from more crime, more street violence and more frequent use of illegal drugs. As well as the direct health effects of these factors, they are likely to lead to a further deterioration in social relations. There will be a rise in tension on the streets, an increased fear of strangers, and a growing concern for security and personal safety. The elderly and others who feel vulnerable will restrict their activities, avoid going out at night and perhaps even cease answering the door bell after dark, if they live alone. Although there has been no research on it, it is possible that people's increased wariness, sense of insecurity and tension may be a widespread health hazard. Whether people feel insecure or fearful only in public places or also when at home alone, if social relations deteriorate to the point where they are predominantly a source of stress, rather than a support in dealing with it, that must have important implications for health.

We have tried to suggest some of the possible ways in which income distribution might exert its influence on health. There are of course numerous other possible pathways. Fortunately establishing causation does not, as people often suggest, mean showing mechanism. In the field of health much the strongest evidence of causation comes from randomised controlled trials which say nothing about mechanism. Thus we knew that aspirin reduced the incidence of heart attacks before anyone knew why, and even where randomised controlled trials were impossible, we knew that smoking caused lung cancer without knowing how. **The statistical evidence on the relationship between income distribution and health is already strong and research on it is continuing. The evidence is however already sufficiently clear for it to be regarded, in analogous medical circumstances, as unethical to withhold treatment.**

If we knew exactly how income redistribution benefitted health it would be a less urgent addition to public health policy than it now is. If its influence could be accounted for wholly in terms of its impact on better known factors such as smoking and diet, it would merely provide an additional way of influencing causes of death over which people already have at least some control. But in fact income redistribution is particularly important because it provides a way of reducing death rates even from causes of death over which we would otherwise have no control. With the exception of lung cancer, preventable risk factors account for comparatively little of most of the major causes of death. Until our knowledge of the aetiology of the degenerative diseases is much better understood it will remain impossible to account for much of the influence income distribution has on death rates. In the meantime we would do well to remember that rather than detracting from the importance we should attach to it, it increases our need to rely on such factors. **That so many causes of death are sensitive to socioeconomic differences may be the most useful thing we know about them.**

4 Public health policies for the future

We hope that by now the reader is convinced of two points. First, the evidence shows increasingly that income differences within countries are the main reason for differences in health both within and between developed countries. Second, the health effects of income distribution can only be dealt with by a redistribution of income. For though in a few cases we know how we could intervene in the causal chain by which income affects health — poor people are more likely to live in damp housing or work in dangerous manual jobs, for example — policies to improve such particular problems would have only a limited impact on health. Inequality seems to be inherently bad for society, particularly for those at the bottom of the pile. Creating a more equal society has to be the main way forward for improvements in public health.

From the public health point of view we have to minimise what the health evidence shows are the socially debilitating effects of inequality. The aim must be to develop a society in which people have a greater sense of security, self-confidence and autonomy. We believe that the fundamental problem is the way status differences lead people to feel devalued, insecure and put at a disadvantage.

Although status divisions take a variety of cultural forms and spring from several different sources, income inequalities are a crucial source and outward expression of these. We believe that the implication of the health evidence is that if the tax/benefit system can be used to reduce income differentials it will have made an important difference to the sense of security and self-confidence in the population at large.

We have no doubt that just as insecurity and loss of self-confidence harm people's health, they also damage people's ability to make an effective productive contribution to society — not only in the realms of paid and unpaid work but also through reducing the quality of their relationships, both personal and with the wider community.

The most urgent need is to bring the incomes of the least well-off up towards the average. But what is the appropriate level of minimum income to aim at? The evidence leads one to expect that increasing the minimum income as a proportion of the average income would go steadily hand in hand with rising health. If this were the case then drawing a poverty line below which no-one should fall would be arbitrary in that the nearer average it is the better for health, and the decision would be based entirely on other political and economic considerations.

There is substantial evidence that the incidence of many different aspects of the deprivation associated with low income does not increase steadily as relative income drops. On the contrary, there seems to be a jump in the degree of deprivation as income drops below around sixty percent of the average. This idea of a threshold level of poverty has been developed by Peter Townsend, originally on data from 1968/9 and although subject to some criticism is on the whole increasingly widely accepted.[46.1] Further support was provided by a MORI survey which found wide agreement on which of a range of items should be considered 'necessities'. Looking at the incomes of those who lacked such 'necessities' they too found a substantial jump in deprivation at around 133% of the then supplementary benefit level.[47] The conclusion of such studies is that to be able to have what people in general regard as 'necessities' in our society, people need an income equivalent to an increase in the state's minimum income (as indicated by benefit levels) of between one-third and one-half, or again to around sixty percent of average household income.

Although we do not fully understand what it is about poverty that damages health, it seems reasonable to expect that such a sharp increase in deprivation would be associated with marked health consequences. There is also some more direct evidence that this level of relative income may be particularly significant in health terms.[4] Thus there are sound reasons for believing that the most urgent part of any effective public health strategy is to ensure that everyone has an income of at least sixty percent of the average.

There is growing concern about the increasing numbers whose poverty excludes them from mainstream society and the social consequences of such marginalisation for society as a whole. There is evidence from opinion polls of widespread belief that the majority should be prepared to make a sacrifice for the minority. But from the point of view of improving health — and probably also the quality of life — this is not an appropriate policy. As we have seen, the evidence is that the health of the poorer two-thirds of the population would benefit from more equal income distribution. Relieving poverty by making life more difficult for those on average incomes is thus a policy of dubious benefit. The money to improve the incomes of the poorest must come not from the majority but from those on high incomes; it will then have benefits for the health of most of the population.

Although this conclusion is attractive for most on the left, recognising the need for it as a public health strategy involves making a major conceptual shift. The fact that inequality influences the health of so many people indicates that it has much deeper health effects than we recognise, way beyond the material risks that have traditionally been seen as the major influences. The psycho-social effects of inequality and differences in social status must be much wider than we are used to recognising.

If the most effective public health strategy is to increase equality and reduce poverty, the key issue for public health then becomes: how should this be achieved?

Focus on tax and benefits

Developing a progressive redistributive tax and benefit policy has to be a top priority. It might seem more attractive to concentrate on inequalities in original income rather than allowing initial inequality and then modifying it. Japan, the country with the greatest equality of net incomes, achieves this largely through limited inequality in gross incomes. Yet there are a number of reasons for making taxes and benefits the main focus of a public health campaign.

Firstly, we can be confident that taxes and benefits can be a tool of redistribution. Economists sometimes argue that using taxes and benefits to redistribute income is doomed to failure as original incomes will automatically adjust to offset any changes. However, a study of income distribution in developed countries in 1979 using the Luxembourg Income Study data found that policies on benefits and direct taxation had a substantial impact on the numbers living in poverty (defined as fifty percent median income adjusted for household size) and was more important than original income in explaining why inequalities in final income are smaller in some countries (such as Sweden) than others (such as the USA).[48] In addition, tax and benefit policy played a major part in the substantial increase in inequality under the Conservative administrations since 1979 and could presumably be equally effective in reversing it.

Secondly, considering original incomes and the many factors that may influence them takes us straight into macro-economics. Ensuring full employment and successful regional policies, calculating the effects of a minimum wage or the impact of training and education on employment levels, deciding whether the growing distinction between 'core' and 'peripheral' workers is here to stay — such questions are vitally important in making original incomes more equal, but they involve discussing policy on almost everything, and require a sophisticated ability to steer through the maze of conflicting views and wishful thinking on the macro-economic effects. Original income can really only be discussed as part of overall economic policy. Whereas government policies on taxes and benefits are rightly seen as concerned primarily with redistribution, this is only one of many factors influencing economic policy.

Thirdly, taxes and benefits have the great advantage of being under direct government control, and having an immediate effect on income. Significant changes can be made in a single budget.

There is a need for policies designed to affect original income and for a strong public health voice in developing such policies. However the public health movement has the greatest chance of successfully influencing redistribution over the next few years by a concerted campaign on taxes and benefits. **We need a heightened awareness that the Chancellor has a much greater impact on health than the Secretary of State for Health, a thought that may well not cross the minds of either.** We need to recognise that the old structure of a department covering both health and social security captured, albeit accidentally, a causal relationship that we must not ignore.

It is appropriate, then, that the remainder of this report is largely devoted to considering proposals for reforming our tax and benefit system. We do not attempt to provide a detailed short-term programme of reform. This has been well done by many others around the poverty lobby and the labour movement. The differences between such schemes are usually either technical — for example whether it is more effective in relieving poverty, let alone improving health, to spend money raising child benefit or increasing retirement pensions — or differences of opinion on the political feasibility of different degrees of redistribution. But alongside these debates about what the early budgets of a Labour government should look like, the whole system of income support is subject to increasing criticism. A top priority for the next Labour government must be to set up an investigation at the highest level into the structure of our tax and benefit systems and how they can best be adapted to meet the needs of the future. Its brief must include the appropriate role, if any, of contribution-related benefits, the main alternative systems particularly social dividends, and reversing the trend towards increasing numbers of claimants and their increasing poverty. It must propose a system that helps people to build their own future, assists the poor but not at the cost of those on average incomes, and can be used as a tool for bringing about a more equal distribution of financial resources throughout society. The rest of this report is devoted to providing some background to such issues.

Dividing the cake

On the face of it, the task seems simple enough. To start with, taking eighteen percent of the disposable incomes (ie after direct taxes and benefits) of the top twenty percent of households by increased taxation would enable a government to double the incomes of the bottom twenty percent through increased benefits. It is important not to lose sight of such simple models when considering the maze of difficulties to their implementation.

But increasing tax revenue from the well-off is not easy. With the help of their accountants and employers they have been shown to have a remarkable ability to re-order their affairs so that increasing their tax rate does not result in a proportional increase the yield. High income tax rates lead to an increase in fringe benefits and other forms of adjustment, as well as direct tax evasion. The ninety eight percent tax rate which could in theory be charged on investment income before 1979 was a notorious failure, filling accountants' pockets rather than the government's. However, increasing tax revenue is perfectly possible, even if not as fast as everyone would like. It requires a combination of broad political support and technical competence. Some of the issues involved are discussed in section 6.

More surprisingly, helping the least well off within our existing structure is not easy either, for a number of reasons, of which the poverty trap is the most glaring. Our system of income support has lagged behind social and political changes, and is now inappropriate. Some hold that it can be rescued, but others, on both right and left, see radical reform of the tax-benefit system as a way to promote social changes. There are clearly limits as to how far this can be done without substantial political support.

How to divide the cake is a central political issue which is a constant source of discussion, struggle and negotiation. There is nothing unique about the transfer of money from the better-off to the poor through taxes and benefits. In all societies some members are engaged in greater production than others and those at less productive stages of their lives — children, sick, disabled and frail people are supported by others — the large majority taking a turn at supporting others at some points in their lives. The feasibility of any such transfer depends on whether the community will cooperate willingly with it. In this context, it is important to recognise the public acceptance of many other cases where resources are redistributed by policies that have remarkably few claims to 'fairness' — for example agricultural subsidies, support for those in higher education, or arts subsidies. Much more costly, if less obviously identified, is the transfer of resources to the better off, for example through concessions for home-owners and tax deductions for business expenses.[46]

Although these are long-standing trends that run through Labour as well as Conservative governments, it is important not to lose sight of how remarkable recent Conservative policy has been. In the words of an ex-researcher to a Conservative MP: *"Until recently it was taken for granted that a proposal involving too many losers was a political non-starter, but events since 1979 have shown otherwise. Losses have become acceptable, provided they are phased in carefully and provided the groups affected are not too powerful."*[49.1]

Fortunately, there is good evidence to suggest that the radical change of government direction in the last ten years is not reflected by changes in public opinion. There are encouraging indications of broad public support for more progressive policies both in relieving poverty and reducing inequality.[50,51,52,53,54] For example the results of the 1990/91 British Social Attitudes Survey, showing that three-quarters of people believe that income differences in Britain are too large, only a quarter thought that large income differences were necessary for national prosperity, sixty three percent support action to reduce income differences and eighty two percent thought that government should spend more on benefits for the poor.[55]

An important note of caution, however, is that evidence of public feeling that the Conservatives have gone too far provides little guide as to the degree of redistribution that would be supported. It is easy for those who do not regard themselves as rich to favour 'the rich' paying more. To hope that redistribution can focus only on millionaires and avoid hitting a broad, well-organised and articulate band of middle-class people who consider themselves decently but not excessively paid, is a chimera, and a dangerous one. Comparatively few individuals are on very high earnings. A ten percent increase in the rate of income tax on incomes over £43,500 would raise only £500 million.[28] Yet a considerable number of households have substantial incomes. Looking at two of the better off household types illustrates this.

Figure 5: Distribution of estimated weekly income 1990

	lowest 10% get less than	lowest 25%	median get exactly	top 25%	top 10% get more than
Total gross household income					
household with 2 adults only	£107.94	£159.13	£285.74	£456.04	£640.84
household with 2 adults and 2 children	196.55	£290	£398.27	£549.59	£714.74
Total disposable household income (ie after tax and benefits)					
household with 2 adults only	£103.83	£147.50	£235.23	£352.50	£482.85
household with 2 adults and 2 children	£165.84	£236.20	£311.81	£428.80	£558.73

1989 figures from the Family Expenditure Survey[56] adjusted for rises in incomes 1989-90

In an effort to woo the middle-class voter the left in Britain has come near to suggesting that taxing the Paul Gettys of the world will alone generate sufficient revenue to finance its policies. A recognition by those in the top twenty five percent that they are indeed privileged and would be financial losers in a progressive redistribution is unavoidable. This is a problem, but one that cannot be dodged and is best faced by direct political debate on the effects of inequality not only on health but on the whole social fabric of society.

5 Reforming social security

"Social security ... is like a game of snakes and ladders played at the Mad Hatter's tea party. Instead of a common starting point some people are not allowed to play at all, some start at the bottom of ladders and others at the top of snakes. The rules change as the game proceeds, snakes turn into ladders and ladders into snakes, and once on a snake it is impossible to escape..."[49.2]

The Beveridge tradition

Social insurance schemes, since their introduction by Bismark, have come to form the backbone of income support throughout Europe. In Britain the Beveridge system, introduced between 1945 and 1948, still provides the framework of income support.

The Beveridge system was designed to tackle what were regarded as the two main causes of poverty. The first was lack of access to a wage — either temporarily, through unemployment or sickness, or permanently, for example through disability or old age. The second was a family size that the wage couldn't cover. For those threatened by poverty due to temporary interruptions from work, or retirement after a lifetime of work, income support was provided through the social insurance system, with eligibility based on contribution record. For others in need who were not eligible for social insurance there would be a residual safety net in the form of means-tested national assistance. To avoid large working families with low wages living in poverty there would be a non-contributory family allowance.

This system still provides the basic framework of our income support. However the British system — and indeed other social security systems throughout Europe — is breaking down.

Firstly, **social security is failing to keep people out of poverty**. By 1979 there was more poverty in Britain than in the fifties, with one in five of the population living in or on the margins of poverty.* This was a miserable achievement for the 34 years since the war, years characterised by considerable economic growth and widespread commitment to the welfare state, exactly half of them under a Labour government.

But since 1979 things have gone from bad to worse. Unemployment has risen, the gap between the well-paid and the low-paid has widened, more of the country's income is paid out as dividends or interest and less as wages, the tax structure has redistributed from poor to rich, high inflation has hit the poor hardest and benefits have risen more slowly than wages.

Together, these changes have resulted in a dramatic increase in inequality at all levels of society. In the first five years under the Conservatives, the top ten percent of families made up all the ground they had lost in the previous twenty years.[28] For the first time since the Second World War, the poorest half of the population have found that their share of total income is dropping.[54] The last decade has been characterised by a substantial rise in earnings, but the improvement of living standards for the average person masks a growing gap between the highest and lowest paid. It is clear that, far from trickling down from rich to poor, household income has been siphoned up from poor to rich.

Not surprisingly, the effects of increased inequality are felt most painfully at the bottom of the pile. In 1987 a quarter of the population were living on low incomes and nearly a fifth — over 10 million people — were living in poverty.[54] **The proportion on low incomes is approximately twice what it was thirty years ago when comparisons are made using an equivalent poverty level**[59]

The poor have not only failed to gain a fair share of increasing prosperity, they have failed to share it at all. Calculating real incomes is controversial but it has been estimated that, since 1979, the poorest ten percent experienced a slight fall in real income after housing costs, while the average income increased by twenty three percent. **The single largest factor in the increase in the numbers in poverty was the Government's decision in 1980 to end indexation of social security benefits to earnings.** It has been calculated that had benefits continued to rise in line with average earnings, by 1990 the number with incomes less than sixty percent of average would have been less than half what it was.[59]

Secondly, despite the increasing poverty of claimants, costs are escalating. Expenditure on social security now amounts to around £1000 a year for each man, woman and child in Britain. As a proportion of gross household income, social security expenditure has risen from eight percent in the mid-sixties to around twelve percent by the end of the eighties.[59] Demographic trends, in particular the increasing number of elderly people, suggest expenditure is unlikely to drop.

Finally, **that part of the system designed as a safety net for those not covered by social insurance is now the main source of benefit for many** Thus in 1988-9 non-contributory benefits came to £21,000 million, compared with almost £20,000 million on national insurance retirement pensions, and just over £6,000 million on other national insurance benefits.[49] By 1986 it was estimated that thirty percent of the population were in families receiving means-tested benefits, and a further ten percent were not claiming benefits they were entitled to.[49] In 1948 when National Assistance was introduced only three percent were reliant on it.[60]

This move away from insurance benefits is due to several changes.

● the increasing numbers of people in need who do not qualify for national insurance benefits;

● the fact that such insurance benefits are often so low that they have to be supplemented by means-tested benefits;

● the failure of child benefit to compensate adequately for additional expenditure, which pushes low-paid families onto means-tested benefits;

- the increased taxation of the low-paid which also has this effect.

Means-testing

Most non-contributory benefits are means-tested. This in itself raises many problems. The basic argument put forward in favour of means testing is that, by removing benefits from those who do not need them, more money is available for those who do. It has been calculated that, for example, cutting universal child benefit by £2.00 would enable an additional £7.70 per child to be given to those on income support and family credit, which redistributes to the poorest thirty percent of families.[28] However, the arguments against means-testing are overwhelming.

Firstly, the assumption that money which is not given to the better-off is available for the poor rests on implausible political assumptions. If removing benefits reduces the net income of the better-off it may be followed by pressure for compensatory tax reductions, reducing the money available for benefits. More important, means testing leaves the interests of the poor dangerously isolated.

There is clear evidence that benefits shared by the middle class were much more successful in retaining their value during the 1980s than those aimed only at the poor[61] even though the government had an explicit policy of tighter targeting.

Secondly, means tests are regarded by many as humiliating, stigmatising and an expression of the notion that income support is a form of charity rather than a right. The conditionality of means tests can significantly restrict personal freedom, for example in the hated cohabitation rule and restriction of earnings.

Thirdly, means-tested benefits are an ineffective way of reaching those in poverty. This is because they are less likely to be claimed by those entitled to them than other benefits. For contributory benefits, such as retirement pension, widow's benefit and unemployment benefit, as well as for child benefit, virtually everyone entitled claims. For the non-means tested One Parent Benefit take up was 93% in 1984. For means-tested benefits the take up rate is much lower. Figures for 1983 and 1984 suggest that of those entitled to claim Supplementary Benefit, only 76% did so, with 77% claiming Housing Benefit, and 54% claiming Family Income Supplement.[28] Once non-take-up is allowed for, it has been calculated that the proposal mentioned earlier to transfer £2 from child benefit to child additions would actually make 62% of families with children in the bottom half of the income distribution worse off![28]

Fourthly, considerable sums are spent administering means-tested benefits, which could otherwise be spent on the benefits themselves. Administering Supplementary Benefit took 11.3% of the benefit expenditure in 1985-6 compared with 1.4% for retirement pensions.[28] Finally, unless the benefit 'taper' is very gradual, claimants suffer all the disadvantages associated with the 'poverty trap', a point discussed later.

In addition, the argument that means-testing is necessary to save government expenditure is totally unconvincing. If there is a genuine concern to save money from within the social security budget the obvious option is to recoup benefits from the better-off through taxation. For example, it has been calculated that if those with incomes over £25,000 had their social security benefits recovered through their tax bill at the end of the year, it would cut net social security expenditure by around ten percent;[59] administration would be cheap and fraud difficult. There is a much more urgent need to look at who is actually benefiting from patterns of expenditure in other areas of public spending such as health care or education, let alone from transport or agricultural policies where 'targeting' the benefits to those most in need could radically alter policies! It is clear that much of the support for means testing, like the obsessive concern with social security fraud, is an expression of fear of people choosing to live 'off the state' when they could be working. It is ironic that this concern has led to proposals that succeed only in discouraging attempts at self-help and trapping people in their role as claimants.

The future of social insurance

Is social insurance, with a means-tested safety net, the best way of organising income support in the future? There are a number of reasons for questioning this.

Above all, it was designed for a world in which the vast majority of people lived in households headed by a wage-earner in full-time work throughout their working life, except for temporary interruptions. This always left some outside the system, but has become increasingly inappropriate. To realise its inadequacy as the basis for a strategy for relieving poverty, it is useful to look at the situation of those in poverty today.

The following table shows the percentage of the ten and a half million people who were living on below fifty percent of average income (after housing costs) in 1987 broken down by situation of head of family.

Figure 6 Percentage of those living on below fifty percent of average income, after housing costs, by situation of head of family.[54]

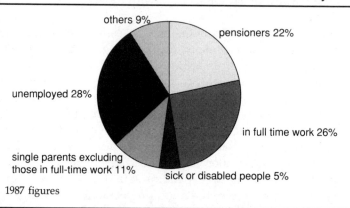

others 9%

pensioners 22%

unemployed 28%

in full time work 26%

single parents excluding those in full-time work 11%

sick or disabled people 5%

1987 figures

Their family situation can been seen by looking at the proportions living in families with various family heads.

Figure 7 Percentage of those living in families with various family heads[54]

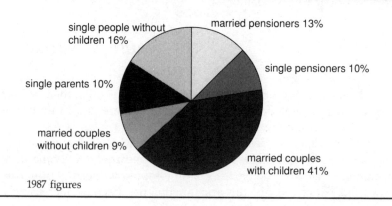

single people without children 16%

married pensioners 13%

single pensioners 10%

single parents 10%

married couples without children 9%

married couples with children 41%

1987 figures

Since 1979 the situation of many of these groups has declined. Pensions and some other benefits have increased in line with prices only and so have dropped still further behind average earnings — some have failed to keep up even with prices. Low pay is more widespread. The proportion of the total adult work-force who are paid less than two-thirds of the median male earnings or hourly equivalent has risen from 36% in 1979 to 45% in 1989/90.[62] Unemployment is less easy to calculate, as the Government has changed the method of calculating the figures thirty times since 1982![54] Although lower than the peak of three million in 1986, unemployment in 1991 is around two million. Households headed by a lone parent are increasing — from 8% of all families with children in 1971 to 14% in 1987 and a high proportion are in poverty.[54]

The social insurance model does not lend itself easily to meeting these changes. It is hard for many — women, single parents, people with disabilities or caring responsibilities — to build up adequate contribution records. It was not designed for helping those in low paid jobs whose wage is insufficient to meet their needs. Long-term unemployment and increasing part-time, casual, temporary and self-employment create more people with inadequate contributions. The return of long-term unemployment has put even adult males outside the system — in 1985 only twenty six percent of unemployed male claimants were in receipt of unemployment benefit.[49] The Institute for Fiscal Studies suggests that two-thirds of the increase in those on supplementary benefit between 1979 and 1987 was due to increased unemployment, through lack of entitlement to unemployment benefit or the need to top it up.[54] Every country in Europe has experienced a similar increase in numbers dependent on benefits but not entitled to social insurance.

A more philosophical issue is that the principle of social insurance embodies a basic distinction between the right to income support, on the one hand, of those who are supporting themselves in the market-place with temporary interruptions and, on the other hand, of those whose contribution through caring for children or adults is unpaid, or whose market-place value is insufficient to earn them a reasonable standard of living. For the latter group, access to income support is given grudgingly, means-tested and withdrawn if there is any possibility of access to a wage — for example by cohabiting. Such values permeate our society and our system of social security both reflects and reinforces them. One consequence of valuing the paid over the unpaid worker is that it diminishes the willingness to perform unpaid work, a factor which is likely to become more significant as opportunities for women to return to work after childrearing increase with the drop in the number of school leavers.

As one critic of the current system put it: *"If you start from the premise that only those people who have been in paid work deserve income security, you create a rat-race society in which people who work for nothing become second-class citizens."*[49.3]

Despite their limitations the introduction of social insurance schemes was a landmark in protecting the poor. But in today's world some commentators have gone so far as to claim that it has come to perpetuate rather than reduce inequalities. The critic who spoke of a 'rat-race society' above, writes: *"Social insurance protects the strong and not-so-strong but leaves the weak dependent on means-tested social assistance or poor relief, and in some countries nothing at all. Today social insurance is getting to look more and more like a select club, from which millions of would-be workers are excluded. Millions more, who do unpaid work in the home or the community, have always been excluded. In the dual labour markets now emerging core workers still stand to benefit from old-style social insurance. But increasing numbers of peripheral workers will be left in the cold and this will affect their future pensions as well as their current living standards."*[49.4]

All in all, it is doubtful whether the current structure, however benevolently implemented, can ensure that no-one is excluded from society by poverty, encourage those who wish to enter the labour market to do so, yet avoid penalising those who are unable to work or who choose to engage in the unpaid tasks of bringing up children or caring. **There is an urgent need for a wide-ranging review of the basis of income support in the future, and a Royal Commission is likely to provide the best format for this**. This is what the Fowler Review promised, yet it failed to examine any of the fundamental tenets of our current system, and indeed by excluding taxation from its brief was precluded from doing so. It is given urgency not only by the difficulties of the current system, some of which (notably the poverty trap) would actually be exacerbated rather than relieved by improving benefit levels, and which will be under increasing strain with the demographic changes underway. In addition, pressure for harmonisation across Europe could too easily lead to the adoption of a virtually immovable framework based on assumptions and values inappropriate for the problems we face and the society we want.

The search for alternatives

Putting forward convincing alternatives is complex. It is not just a matter of having the political will to find the necessary money

— there are important technical problems, and complex social and political implications, to be considered. The main conclusion of almost all commentators is that there is no ready-made obvious solution waiting to be adopted. With benefits, as in so many other areas, Conservative attacks have diverted those who should have been at the forefront of developing alternatives to the existing system into frustrating campaigns to defend it. Nonetheless, the debate about more major reform is becoming increasingly sophisticated — helped by the development of better computer modelling.

The majority of proposals put forward by both the liberal and socialist left, sometimes labelled the 'Beyond Beveridge' approach, aim to build on the best elements of the current system, and to coordinate benefits and taxation.[63,64,28,60] Labour Party policy also fits this model.[65] Benefit proposals are put forward as part of a package with redistributive tax reform. They usually retain a commitment to maintain or extend social insurance, though there have been suggestions[64] of eliminating the contributory principle altogether, and sometimes proposals are couched in the short-to-medium term, stressing the need for a wide-ranging discussion on the long-term basis of income support. (The CPAG pamphlet *There is an Alternative* is an example.) The general aim is to reverse the trend towards selectivist, means-tested residual benefits, and increase non-means-tested benefits based on 'contingency' — such as unemployment or disability. The most immediate tasks are usually seen as increasing contribution-based benefit rates, taking a large number out of means-testing, raising children's scale-rates and child benefit, restoring indexation to the higher of wages or prices and removing discrimination against the long-term unemployed and younger claimants.

There are also a wide range of schemes put forward for various contingent benefits, aimed at people with disabilities, carers, mothers of young children and other groups aimed in part at reducing means-testing — though housing support proves stubbornly difficult in this respect. A principle that is increasingly adopted is that changes should aim to make the system neutral with respect to formal marriage, sexual orientation, illegitimacy and family breakdown, and to maximise choices such as those between, for example, paid employment and childcare or caring. Developing and modelling the impact of detailed proposals, either overall or in part, has been a main focus of activity of those aiming at a social security system that both relieves and prevents poverty.

Others, however, feel that such proposals are just tinkering with a structure that is irreparably flawed and must be redesigned from scratch. The two main alternatives (other than proposals for a 'minimal state' from the new right) are negative income tax and some form of social dividend. They have many similarities but approach the problems from very different standpoints. For the left, social dividends prove by far the most interesting, and are attracting increasing attention, partly around the work of the Basic Income Research Group associated with the National Council of Voluntary Organisations. Such schemes are often misunderstood, and raise important issues of principle and general policy. But before moving on to the details of such schemes it is necessary to be clear about one of the fundamental issues behind discussions of reforms, marginal 'tax' rates and the poverty trap.

Marginal 'tax' rates and the poverty trap

The tax and social security systems have grown up independently, creating unplanned interactions of which the 'poverty trap' is the best-known. The poverty trap is the way in which the poor can find themselves little if any better off if they earn more (although sometimes the term is restricted to those situations where increased earnings leave people worse off). They face very high marginal 'tax' rates — that is to say only a small proportion of the next pound earned (which may also be the first pound earned) goes into the earner's pocket, the rest being removed as tax, national insurance contribution or through benefit withdrawal.

The marginal 'tax' rate can in some situations be over 100% as in the classic poverty trap — ie a higher gross income can result in a lower net income — and there may be 'steps' as entitlement to flat-rate benefits, such as free school meals, are withdrawn at a particular level.

If the combined effect of the tax and benefit system is to be redistributive, then it is inevitable that some people will find an increase in gross income is accompanied by a less-than- proportional increase in net income. The poverty trap is the result of concentrating this process on comparatively few people towards the bottom of the income scale rather than spreading the burden more widely, and on those better able to afford it. Many people are surprised to realise that, for the majority of the population, marginal 'tax' rates go down as income increases. Using 1989 figures, low-earners who are also receiving benefits, can face marginal 'tax' rates over 90%. For the majority of wage-earners, in the band of income between withdrawal of means-tested benefits and the upper limits for National Insurance contribution, the rate falls to 34%. Once the National Insurance ceiling is reached, the marginal 'tax' rate becomes the rate of income tax — initially at 25%, then on incomes of around £500 a week (depending on mortgage and other tax reliefs) at 40%.

The marginal 'tax' rates of most earners are thus kept down at the expense of very high marginal 'tax' rates for those on benefits. This is politically expedient; claimants are powerless and few in number compared with tax-payers, and their 'right' to their benefits is valued much less highly than the 'right' to earned income. Historically, the poverty trap was an acute problem facing a few families. The 1988 budget succeeded in abolishing marginal 'tax' rates of over 100%, but did so by turning the poverty trap into a less extreme problem facing larger numbers of families.[49]

The disincentive effect of high marginal 'tax' rates was the government's justification for the abolition, in the 1988 Budget, of the top rate of income tax of 60% (which would have affected 180,000 families in 1988-9). But the April 1988 benefit reforms increased to 545,000 the number of low income families facing marginal 'tax' rates of 70% or more.[28] And, although there is little evidence that marginal 'tax' rates affect the employment decisions (rather than just the financial arrangements) of the rich, for the poor they are much more important. When the costs of working, including transport, clothing and — most importantly for many — childcare, are taken into account, working may not be economic.

In broad terms, an income support system that encourages people to work within the formal economy if they wish to must be preferable to one which makes working not worthwhile or pushes people into illegality. Ensuring that claimants do not face very high marginal 'tax' rates is essential to this.

Social dividends and negative income tax

Negative income tax would work more or less like income tax does now, with a similar calculation made for everyone. Those below the tax threshold, whether earning or not, would receive payments instead of making them. With a social dividend, also known as a basic income or convertible tax credit, everyone would receive a certain income through the state whatever their employment status, and all other income would be taxed, with no allowances. In both systems, taxes and benefits are calculated together and everyone is guaranteed a minimum income. The safety net is there, as a right, for everyone rather than, as at present, having a means-tested safety net only for those who fall outside more standard schemes.

Social dividends do not mean that everyone gets a uniform cash hand-out whether they need it or not. For most of the population they are a tax credit or allowance, paid as cash, but for those who cannot take advantage of this they can be converted into cash benefit. Perhaps the clearest way of understanding this model is to consider child benefits, which are in fact a partial social dividend or convertible tax credit. For those above the tax threshold child benefit effectively lowers their net tax bill compared with childless people on the same income, though this is received as a cash allowance rather than through PAYE or tax returns as was the child tax allowance that child benefit replaced. The great advantage, of course, is that those who do not earn enough to benefit from tax allowances still receive the cash payment. In effect, a social dividend switches automatically between being a benefit to being an income tax allowance as the receiver's income varies.

There are two major differences between social dividends and negative income tax. The first concerns their effectiveness in dealing with the poverty trap and those just above the minimum income. A pure social dividend scheme eliminates the poverty trap — the marginal 'tax' rate is the same for everyone (until higher income tax bands are reached) and working, however little, is always worth it. Negative income tax schemes may avoid the worst excesses of the poverty trap but they institutionalise a more moderate version of it. It is an attempt to target money on those in most need at any moment, bringing them up to a minimum income, while regarding any benefits to those above this as unnecessary. While possibly effective in relieving poverty, it does nothing to help people to escape from it in the future by encouraging employment. Social dividends on the other hand, while they do not necessarily offer a higher standard of living to those with no earnings, do offer the opportunity of legally building on the minimum in a way that can help people escape from poverty in the longer term.

Payments under negative income tax are administratively complex. They would have to be processed as situations changed. It would have difficulty in coping with those moving in and out of employment through the year; if someone loses their job, it is not adequate to assure them that when they return to work, their tax payments will be lower — they need an income immediately. It becomes administratively very complex if people are to have money as soon as they need it; experimental systems in the USA placed the onus on claimants to file claims, which would undoubtedly miss some of those in need.

Social dividends, by contrast, are simple to administer. They have the advantage — most important to the poor — of providing a regular income irrespective of how other income might fluctuate. It might at first sight seem rather clumsy to have taxpayers paying tax that is then repaid to them in the form of a flat-rate benefit, but in fact it is administratively extremely efficient to have a payment credited through, for example, the post office or to a bank account at a rate that would change only rarely (for example on having a child or becoming disabled) and taxes paid through the income tax system, where speed is less vital.

Overall, a social dividend offers much more potential for those concerned with poverty prevention and redistribution than negative income tax. It can be applied in many different ways: the unit of selection could be the individual, family or household, it is compatible with minimum wage or its absence, levels of payment could depend on factors related to need such as disability, it can be applied only to those who meet particular criteria such as pensioners, those with disabilities, or carers. Receipt can be made conditional on willingness to participate in the labour market for those without other responsibilities.

A major argument against a full social dividend is the cost of providing a reasonable standard of living for those with no earnings. An important aim of tax and benefits is to ensure that it is financially worth-while taking part time or casual work. Since earnings are liable either for tax or for benefit withdrawal, any earnings reduce the costs of such schemes, but if marginal 'tax' rates are too high they undermine much of their rationale. Yet if the marginal 'tax' rate on the first band of earned income is low, very large numbers of people not usually regarded as poor will be receiving more in their guaranteed income than they are paying in taxes. For example, if the social dividend was £50 a week and income tax started at 20%, anyone with a gross weekly income of less than £300 (£15,600 pa) would be a net beneficiary. This makes the scheme astronomically expensive, and explains why the guaranteed minimum income that can be provided for a given cost is low. What makes some of the social dividend schemes so much more expensive than conventional benefit systems is not primarily more generous benefits to non-earners, but the reduced marginal 'tax' rates for those at the bottom of the earnings distribution.**

In addition to the cost, the scale of changes, both administrative and political, involved in introducing full social dividends are such that it is widely accepted as unrealistic to attempt to introduce them over the life of one parliament (see [49, 66]). It is unlikely that they would ever be introduced if they were nothing more than a party-political football. They would need solid backing, maybe in the form of the conclusions of a Royal Commission, wide professional and public support, and a degree of cross-party sympathy.

Phasing in integration

Thus for both financial and political reasons, full social dividends are currently dismissed by virtually all commentators as an option for the near future. Detailed discussion has focused on models of partial integration — that is, either a low level of social dividend topped up with other benefits, or a higher level for some members of the community only, such as pensioners or people with disabilities. In this way integration could be phased in, initially as a fairly small part of the total, eventually allowing the phasing out of other benefits.

Phasing in integration has a number of advantages. First, protecting some existing rights for a time may be both equitable and politically expedient. Second, phasing in gives public opinion time to change. Third, it would also allow the possibility of using any economic growth to reduce the impact on losers, and thus their opposition. Fourth, administrative difficulties would be reduced. Many critics of radical changes say their introduction would be an administrative nightmare. Against this it has been argued that the difficulties consist largely in the many civil servants whose livelihood is tied up in the cumbersome administration of the current system. However, the civil service is an opponent to avoid, so it would be preferable to allow time for natural wastage and avoid mass redundancies. Fifth, computerising the system has been estimated to take around five years.[49]

Social dividends raise a number of wider social issues, and it is on these, at least as much as the technical difficulties, that attitudes are determined. A full social dividend scheme offers the prospect of a system that operates in a way that makes no distinction between net contributors and net receivers, is unconditional in its support and aims to maximise the opportunities for people to sort out their lives in different, and changing, ways. For many, this is the greatest attraction. But there is no doubt that some are stirred into passionate objection to the idea that men and women who could work are getting something without working for it — despite the fact that the current system actively discourages them from taking paid work or training, unless they are in the position to command a well-paid full time job.

In part, the issue is an empirical one; would social dividends act as a disincentive to employment and can the economy afford this? It also relates to broader social issues, particularly what future is envisaged for the current distinction between paid and unpaid work and the role and status of women, of elderly people and of those with disabilities. Such questions take us back to our fundamental concerns with security and self-esteem that appear to have such an influence not only on health but on the wider quality of life of all of us.

---

* The two standard definitions of poverty are to be on incomes at or below fifty percent average income (adjusted for household size and composition) or the state minimum income as laid down by benefit levels. Low income, or 'on the margins of poverty' is defined as at or below sixty percent of average income (again adjusted) or 140% of benefit levels. Both are clearly measures of relative poverty, and give similar results. For a discussion of the differences between these measures, see[54]

It is generally agreed that poverty figures underestimate the extent of poverty. First, they normally exclude homeless people and those living in institutions such as hospitals, nursing homes, residential care and prisons. Such people usually have very little money, which compounds the extreme exclusion from participation in society that they experience for other reasons.

Second, changes in the government's basis of analysis, from families to households, will miss some in poverty. It has been estimated that this change may result in 1.5 million less people appearing in the government statistics as in poverty.[54]

Third, an important and usually ignored aspect of poverty is poverty within families. There is evidence that some women deprive themselves in order to protect other members of the household, and that some men keep money for themselves.[57] A series of studies have found that between a fifth and a third of women whose marriages had broken down and were on social security reported that they were 'better off' than when living with their husbands, even when their previous family income was well above benefit levels.[49] It is thus highly likely that poverty amongst women is more widespread than figures on family or household income would suggest.[58] The way in which benefits are paid, or tax is deducted, can of course affect this; it is a widely recognised advantage of paying child benefit to the mother and there is no reason why all benefits should not be paid individually, even if assessed jointly.

** Generally, negative income tax schemes work out cheaper for the same level of guaranteed minimum income, as benefit withdrawal rates below the break-even levels are usually higher than the rates of positive taxation above them. This offers the opportunity to keep costs down by reducing benefits to those just above the minimum income level who are considered not to need them, albeit at the cost of high marginal 'tax' rates, thus defeating one of the main aims of integration. (The Adam Smith Institute negative income tax scheme, for example, is not unusual in having a 90% benefit withdrawal rate.[49]) Withdrawing benefits faster than tax is imposed also retains the traditional distinction between taxpayers and beneficiaries. Perhaps for this reason as well as lower cost it has traditionally attracted more supporters in high places than have social dividends.[49]

*** A number of different proposals for partial integration have been made. Parker[49] contains a useful analysis of five schemes for partial social dividends, including her own preferred option, Basic Income 2000, which includes a full social dividend for pensioners, people with disabilities and carers. Her discussion should convince anyone not only that integration can serve different political ends, but that political good-will is not a sufficient criterion with which to engage in this debate; designing a system, whether integrated or based on the current dual set-up, which actually has the effects desired is highly complex and indeed in some cases desirable ends are incompatible.

6 *Reforming taxation*

Tax is an important determinant of inequality for two reasons; first, it is a major factor in the distribution of income and wealth in the country, and is directly responsible for poverty in some instances. Second, any proposal to reduce poverty and inequality by improving benefits must answer the question — can more money be raised by taxation without being too unpopular, causing widespread evasion, and damaging the economy? It would be rash to assume that money can be made available from elsewhere in the government budget while there are so many areas of public expenditure in need of funds. Tax levels influence health in a number of ways additional to their redistributive effect, most obviously through the level of public services that can be supported. Here, however, we are discussing only the impact of tax on the distribution of personal financial resources.

Tax reform is a complex area. Understanding the real effects of the present system, let alone accurately predicting the impact of changes, is a major task. This section outlines some of the issues that arise in creating a more redistributive tax system, in particular when taxing income and health. We have excluded the topical controversy over local taxes as it is well covered elsewhere.

Tax changes since 1979

The Conservative government talks a lot about the need to reduce the level of taxation. In fact, they have slightly increased the proportion of national income taken by taxation. The illusion of lower taxes is largely the result of a shift in patterns of taxation from income tax to less visible taxes such as VAT. The ill-fated poll tax was an instance of a wider trend.

A series of Conservative budgets have reduced the tax paid by the rich. The 1988 Budget was a watershed in redistributing from the poor to the rich, abolishing all but one of the higher tax rates, leaving 95% of taxpayers on the basic rate, and giving other generous tax cuts to the better-off.[28] Although the total effect of Conservative budgets has been to cut direct taxes, in the words of one commentator: *"Remarkably, what has happened has been a virtually zero net cost reform; the cuts in direct taxes have been entirely paid for by cuts in the generosity of benefits.... There has, however, been a major redistribution from those on low incomes to the better off.... The losses [resulting from changes since 1979] for the bottom fifty percent average out at nearly £8.50 per family, while the top ten percent have gained nearly £40 per family."*[28.1]

Reforming income tax

There are two basic ways of making income tax more progressive without reducing revenue — increasing personal allowances or introducing graduated levels of income tax. Larger allowances paid for by raising the basic tax rate bring slightly greater benefits to the poorest taxpayers but leave large numbers on middle incomes worse off and raise marginal tax rates. Most taxpayers would still pay a flat rate. A graduated system has the advantage that the tax reductions for those on low incomes are paid for by the better off rather than those on average incomes. This is preferable from a health point of view, and is politically more acceptable, in that fewer people are worse off. The UK is unusual in not having a graduated structure. Of the 19 OECD countries in 1988 the UK was unique in having as few as two tax bands;

Belgium had thirteen, France and Japan twelve, and West Germany a graduated curve. The UK also has lower marginal tax rates on top incomes than any country except Switzerland.[28]

It is tempting to hope that gaining access to very high incomes could raise substantial revenue without the need for large tax increases for those on above average earnings, including the articulate and politically powerful people on professional and middle managerial incomes. However, this is unfortunately wishful thinking, for two reasons. First, the very rich are likely to be able to arrange their finances to make them less liable to tax if marginal tax rates get very high. It has proved remarkably hard to extract high tax rates from those who can afford good accountants. Second, people on professional incomes are comparatively richer than they recognise. As Hills puts it: *"Someone earning 1.5 times average earnings does not sound very rich, but they are within the top 10% of the earnings distribution. Someone on 'twice average earnings' (just over £25,000 in 1988-9) is within the top 3% of the earnings distribution. Such people do not think of themselves as amongst the very rich."*[28.2]

Raising tax rates for those with significantly but not massively above average incomes is a nettle that has to be grasped; graduated tax bands are the obvious way to do it. In theory, income tax allowances should prevent the lower paid from paying tax on the income they need to avoid poverty. In fact, allowances are of more value to the better off for two reasons.

First, they are worth more to high-rate taxpayers; because they reduce the amount of taxable income, less will be taxed at the higher rate. An additional allowance of £1 is worth £25 to a basic rate taxpayer, £40 to someone paying at 40%. This would become an increasing problem if graduated tax bands were introduced. Restricting personal allowances to the basic rate, through a tax credit or zero-rat system, as has now been done for mortgages, overcomes this problem. In either case revenue would increase as higher rate taxpayers would pay more and some taxpayers would be pushed into a higher rate.

Second, those with higher incomes make more use of many allowances, such as mortgage relief and pension concessions. This is becoming increasingly important. The cost of mortgage interest tax relief grew at a staggering nine hundred percent between 1960 and 1985.[49.5] The Business Expansion Scheme, Personal Equity Plans, Enterprise Zones and concessions for share options have been introduced recently and benefit mainly the rich. Because of the scale of allowances, they have a major impact on tax levels. They are officially estimated to reduce the income tax base (the proportion of income on which tax is paid) by over fifty percent[49] leading to much higher tax rates. Allowances could be limited by a minimum tax, as exists in the USA, or by a maximum allowance (which if it were not raised with inflation would gradually widen the tax base.)

A number of countries give 'single-earner' tax relief to support families while one parent is looking after children. But it is a clumsy and inefficient tool for achieving an aim which would be much better met by focusing directly on the costs of children (for example by child benefit) or of lost job opportunities.

Taxation of married women has long been a muddle. Until recently working married women were penalised. The government's new system, allowing independent taxation but still retaining a tax benefit for being married, reverses this and favours married couples over unmarried ones. Without this aim, there is no justification for retaining additional tax relief for being married. On the principle that the state should not subsidise one pattern of family relationships rather than another, the fairest arrangement would seem to be completely independent taxation, with no married man's allowance but compensated by an increase in Child Benefit. This is even-handed between married and unmarried couples, heterosexual or homosexual, men and women.

In conclusion, making income tax significantly more progressive is relatively straightforward, though phasing in would be necessary in a number of areas. Converting the personal allowance to a zero rate band, given to everyone irrespective of marital status, and introducing a graduated rate structure with a lower starting-point and higher top rate than at present, should provide the main framework. Increasing the tax base by reducing tax concessions is discussed below.

National Insurance Contributions

National Insurance Contributions are even less progressive than income tax. The effect of going above the lower earnings limit for insurance contributions is that earners suddenly pay contributions on all their income, not just on the amount above the limit, which could be avoided by a zero-rate band. The maximum contribution means that those with higher incomes pay a smaller proportion of their income in contributions, which is clearly regressive. There is currently an incentive for employers to keep earnings down below the threshold.

Replacing employers contributions by a payroll tax would avoid this. A number of people have proposed combining income tax and national insurance contributions into one system. There are many ways in which this is logical. However, it should be considered as part of a wider discussion about the future of social insurance.

In the meantime, **a zero-rate band with a flat or graduated percentage above this, abolishing the upper earnings limit, would provide a more progressive basis for employee's contributions, and a payroll tax for employers would have a beneficial effect on employment practice.**

Company taxes

It is difficult to know who ends up bearing the costs of company taxes, and thus to estimate the effect. If it is the shareholders, such taxes would be progressive; if the consumers they would operate like other indirect taxes and tend to be regressive. The latter becomes more likely as investment is increasingly international, so a lower rate of return results in less willingness to invest. But it may be difficult to pass on costs to consumers if imported goods do not carry these costs. It would be hard for one country to raise its rates above those of its rivals. But rates of company tax in the UK are lower than almost all other developed countries, at 35% in 1988 compared with rates over 50% in West Germany, Sweden, Japan and Denmark.[28] It is however somewhat misleading to compare rates without also comparing the tax base. In this situation, company taxes could be an easy way for the government to raise revenue — precisely because it is not clear who pays them, they cause little protest. It is interesting to note that Japan, with the most egalitarian income distribution in the developed world, has low rates of personal taxation compensated for by high company taxes.

Indirect taxes

The UK raises a higher proportion of tax revenue from indirect taxes than any other OECD country.[28] Indirect taxes tend to be regressive, as better-off people save more, but in Britain this is not true of VAT because of the zero-rating of a number of 'essentials' and the exemption of housing. VAT in fact takes a slightly smaller proportion of the disposable income of poorer households than of the richest.[28] There is a move within the EC to 'harmonise' VAT rates (largely to avoid cross border shopping) which would involve charging VAT on most zero-rated goods. **This would be markedly regressive and would have a significant impact on the poorest families. This requires vigorous opposition. If VAT rates are to be harmonised, it should be by extending the benefit of zero-rating essentials to other countries.**

Two other indirect taxes, on alcohol and tobacco, have obvious direct health implications, as consumption of both is highly price-sensitive. Alcohol tax takes least from the poorest twenty percent of households and around the same proportion from the rest. Harmonisation within the EC would involve a very substantial reduction in tax on wine and beer (estimated to result in increasing consumption by around a third) and a smaller reduction in tobacco tax.

Tobacco tax is highly regressive. This poses an obvious dilemma. Major expenditure is involved. The poorest fifth as a whole spend 4.3% of their disposable income on tobacco tax, but as less than half of such households have a smoker in them, in those that do expenditure averages a staggering 9%![28] If there were effective ways of discouraging smoking other than by price, there would be a strong case for adopting them in preference.

Wealth

Wealth is a source of income, both in cash (for example from investments) and kind (such as the value of living in a house). The possibility of spending the capital opens up a range of alternatives in times of crisis and when making major life decisions. Equally important, the knowledge that such capital is there to be drawn on if necessary can make a substantial difference to the quality of life (and so to health), freeing people from constant fears about the lack of options they would face in an emergency. **The increase in choice and in ability to plan for the future and deal with the unexpected, are benefits of wealth that are underestimated in comparison with its ability to generate higher consumption levels.**

Wealth is even more unequally distributed than income. The richest five percent of the population own forty percent of the wealth.[28] The richest ten percent and twenty five percent increased their proportion of total wealth between 1976 and 1988, whether the value of dwellings is included or excluded.[67]

Since 1979 the Conservatives have reduced taxes on wealth. Investment income surcharge has been abolished, and capital gains have had their tax liability reduced in a number of significant ways, although at least those on higher tax rates now pay capital gains at the higher rate. Inheritance tax liability is reduced; the threshold has increased much faster than inflation and tax is now a flat rate (40%) rather than a graduated one which benefits the largest fortunes.

Taxing wealth is an obvious approach to redistributing resources within society. There are two aspects to taxing wealth — taxing the income generated by ownership of wealth, and taxing wealth directly.

Taxing unearned income

Most of the benefits of wealth ownership come in forms which are not taxed. One might expect wealth to give a nominal 'rate of return' (ie ignoring inflation) of around ten percent. In fact, the total amount of declared 'investment income' and capital gains assessed for tax suggests an absurdly low rate of return of only one percent.[28] **Attention needs to focus not only on the rate of taxation of such taxable returns, but on increasing the proportion of the benefits of wealth ownership that are taxed, ie the tax base.**

The current system is a mass of contradictions; the return on different forms of investment is taxed in very different ways. At one extreme, someone owning a house with a mortgage receives tax relief on their mortgage repayments, the 'income in kind' of living in the house rent-free is not taxed, nor is the increase in the value of their house over time (the capital gain). Share option schemes, Business Expansion Schemes, older life insurance contracts and pension contributions are also dealt with by the tax system in a way which makes them better than tax-free. Those who can afford a good accountant can, by careful management making the best of such schemes and taking advantage of capital gains allowances on shares and other concessions, pay little or no tax while reaping a considerable income. On the other hand, the investments most likely to be held by those with small savings — building society and bank deposits and gilts, pay a rate of tax that (unlike capital gains on shares) makes no allowance for inflation and is paid even by non-tax-payers. **Thus the richest are likely to be paying tax on capital at the lowest rate, and small savers at the highest.**

In addition, investment income is generally treated more favourably than earned income. Earned income pays the marginal income tax rate and the National Insurance Contribution. The only investments at a higher rate of tax will be those — such as building society accounts — where no allowance is made for inflation, in times when inflation is high. An investment income surcharge equivalent to the employees national insurance contribution is often advocated to eliminate this anomaly and raise revenue (cushioning the effect on pensions).

Debate about reforming this untidy and inequitable system has generally been dominated by two models:

- **Comprehensive income tax**, in which all sources of income, whether earned, fringe benefits, dividends and interest, or the value of goods owned (such as the value to owner-occupiers of living in their own house) are taxed at the same rate. (This may of course have a progressive rate schedule depending on total income).

- **Expenditure tax**, in which the tax base would be income minus savings and plus expenditure from savings, ie the total amount spent in a year. This is similar to the way in which pensions contributions are tax deductible and pensions are taxable.

Neither of these schemes is straightforward.[28] Comprehensive Income Tax involves considerable administrative difficulties that are not easily overcome. Expenditure Tax causes concern about the negative effect on the government's tax flow, lack of progressiveness, the interaction with company tax, and the difficulties that might arise for a country that introduced the scheme when surrounding countries had not. For these reasons the interest now is largely in more piecemeal action, aiming to capture a notion of 'fairness' in making the tax treatment of different forms of income more equal. One such programme for short-term action is put forward by Hills for the Child Poverty Action Group,[28] and discussed further at the end of this section. It aims to increase the tax revenue from the benefits of wealth ownership by removing particularly advantageous tax arrangements, such as the Business Expansion Scheme, share option schemes, Life Assurance Premium Relief and mortgage relief on higher rates of tax. Capital Gains Tax should be given more bite, for example by removing the £5000 tax free allowance. The tax-free status of pension fund income should be investigated.* Investment Income should be surcharged to bring it into line with tax on earnings (pensioners who had opted for savings giving interest rather than pensions could be safeguarded).

These suggestions are all comparatively straightforward and could be introduced quite quickly. In the longer term, moving towards taxing unearned income more heavily than earnings seems equitable, though small savers and high earners may point to the need for exceptions.

An important and controversial issue is that of home ownership. Owner-occupation is undoubtedly very much higher than it would be without the support it has received from the tax system. The cost of mortgage interest tax relief in 1986/7 was around £4.5 billion, about the same as the cost of housing benefit, even before the value of imputed rents is considered. If the aim of providing financial help for housing costs is to support those in need, this is clearly inefficient and it would be equitable to give help irrespective of whether a property is rented or owner-occupied. But mortgage relief was designed to encourage increased owner-occupation, not relieve poverty.

Clearly, financial support for housing costs needs to be positioned within a wider housing policy. Housing is an important aspect of inequality in our society and housing policy needs to address this directly, as well as using the tax and benefits system to ensure that people are not subjected to hardship through inability to meet their housing costs. The division between the majority of the population who live in their own homes and have a substantial inheritance to leave behind them, and the minority who, through necessity rather than choice in most cases, rent their homes, would not disappear by improving the quality or quantity of neglected public housing, vital though this is. Should socialists regard owner-occupation as an important way of giving people control over their own lives that should be made widely available to poorer households? Or should they retain their traditional preference for public housing, albeit with a less bureaucratic and more democratic form of management, regarding home ownership as inherently divisive and individualising? If so, what policy should be adopted towards the two-thirds of households that own their own homes now?

An obvious approach to the immediate problems is to phase out mortgage relief and perhaps to tax the value of living in a house. If relief on mortgages were abolished, house prices would go down, (the capitalisation effect) so it is not necessarily the case that less people would be able to afford to buy in the long run, although there would be considerable hardship if this was introduced overnight. The value of living in a house (the 'imputed rent') was subject to income tax until 1963 and is a major benefit of house ownership.

Direct taxation of wealth

Taxing wealth directly provides a complementary approach to that of taxing income from wealth. It is essential for the creation of a more egalitarian society that concentrated wealth should be dispersed and the benefits of security and choice that accrue from even quite small amounts of capital should be more widely distributed. It is tempting to think that substantial revenue could be raised, and redistributed to the poorest, by taxing the wealth of the rich. Unfortunately, this is no simple matter.

The two basic approaches are to tax ownership of wealth directly, usually on an annual basis, and to tax wealth as it is transferred between people through death or gifts. A number of countries, including Austria, Denmark, France, Ireland, the Netherlands, Norway Spain, Sweden, and West Germany have a wealth tax. Their experience has, on the whole, not been encouraging. A major problem is the cost of administration in relation to yield — and it is worth the rich investing heavily in tax avoidance techniques. Tax on capital transfers seems more attractive — as Hills notes: *"If wealth changes hands every generation — say, every 25 years — a tax at 25% on transfer would raise as much as a 1% annual wealth tax. Not only would one only have to cope with 4% of the number of cases each year, but they would also be easier; those receiving transfers have an interest in establishing legal ownership, making the wealth easier to identify."*[28.3]

Taxes on transferring capital have traditionally been a much more important source of revenue than they are today. Eighty years ago, estate duty raised twenty percent of tax revenue (excluding customs duties); the figure today is under one percent. The Thatcher government's introduction of a flat rate Inheritance Tax and a number of concessions benefit those inheriting large fortunes most, and mean that *"the prospects of living on inherited wealth are now brighter than they have been for many years"*.[28.3]

Currently Inheritance Tax is paid at a flat rate on the total estate. This could be made more progressive by returning to a graduated system so that larger estates paid a higher rate of tax. An alternative approach is to tax the receipt of wealth, graduated according to the amount received. One variant is a Lifetime Accessions Tax, where tax is paid according to the accumulated amount of gifts and bequests received over a lifetime — perhaps allowing a certain amount tax free, and graduated tax rates thereafter. Another variant is to count gifts and bequests as income, on which income tax is paid. In both cases, someone with wealth to leave will have an incentive to spread it amongst a number of people rather than leaving it to one person. Although this would tend to reduce revenue, it also helps to encourage the spread of wealth to a wider group, albeit largely the already better-off. This is usually regarded as socially beneficial, though there are those who argue that giving more of the population middle-class interests leaves those who do not share in this process increasingly marginalised and can work against reducing inequality.**

The basic disadvantage of taxing wealth on inheritance is that redistribution is so slow. It takes a generation until all wealth has been taxed even once. But without major political changes that could make the current distribution of wealth seem totally unacceptable and overthrow existing patterns of ownership in a radical way, it may in practice prove the most effective way available.

Conclusion

There is general agreement over a number of short-term reforms that could make the existing tax system considerably more progressive and raise additional revenue for increased benefits. However, the regressive redistribution of a decade of Conservative governments is so great that discussion of short-term measures is usually couched in terms of getting back to a situation which is overall no worse than that in 1979! Sometimes even this is considered too ambitious. The proposal by *Breadline Britain 1990s* for a 5p increase in income tax, which is assumed to be about the maximum that is politically acceptable, is designed to reduce poverty only to the 1983 level.[51] The Labour Party policy document[65] suggests a fairly standard package of measures, but without details of tax rates and bands it is not possible to work out the redistributive impact. However, the stress on the need to move gradually so as not to disrupt family budgets, combined with a tendency to hope that economic growth will be sufficient to ensure that real losses can be avoided for all except the very rich, suggests that even returning to 1979 levels of inequality might be no speedy task.

Hills[28] offers a package that has been widely influential. He sets out a modestly progressive strategy for tax reform which is designed to be comparatively easy to introduce both administratively and politically. Most people gain and it can be seen to accord with acceptable notions of 'fairness'. He points out the conflict between redistribution on the one hand, and ensuring that as many people as possible gain to secure widespread political support on the other. His specific aim is the modest one of reversing the distributive effects of the changes to the direct tax and benefit systems that have taken place since 1979, at the same time eliminating anomalies and creating a fairer foundation to build on in the future and at a cost comparable to the government's proposals.

Suggested tax reforms include:

- a graduated income tax structure rising to 50%;

- the conversion of Income Tax Allowances into a Zero Rate Band;

- fully independent taxation with no special allowance for married men offset by doubling Child Allowance and an increase in the married pension.

- re-introduction of an investment income surcharge;

- restriction or removal of various unprogressive concessions and allowances, with the reduction or phasing out of mortgage relief and relief on private pensions;

- progressive structures for employee National Insurance Contributions, with abolition of the upper limit and converting the lower limit into an allowance.

Although income tax rate increases for the better-off would be moderate, increased National Insurance Contributions, investment income surcharge and a substantial widening of the tax base would increase substantially the amount of tax they paid. Clearly the effect of such a package depends on the levels at which taxes and benefits are set. Hills suggests levels that will benefit 73% of families, with only 23%, almost all those on the highest incomes, losing. At these levels the scheme costs about the same as current government proposals. Although average marginal tax rates are slightly increased for men (though reduced for women) the number on marginal rates over 70% (ie low earners) is substantially reduced. This is achieved within a tax structure which incorporates a top marginal tax rate on earnings of 61.5% and of 65% on investment income — well within the mainstream of other European countries.

Greater redistribution through these parts of the tax system would involve accepting higher tax rates, more losers or both, but would not put Britain outside the European range. Even without this, there is scope for further redistribution by a progressive method of local taxation, greater taxation of wealth and inheritance, and reformed taxation of savings, as well as ensuring that indirect taxation does not hit the poorest, which involves at least safeguarding zero-rated VAT.

Such a scheme shows that it is possible to achieve four important objectives simultaneously by reform of the existing personal tax system. One could fund substantial increases in benefits, make the tax system itself more progressive and more logical in structure, ensure that a large majority of the population would gain, and financially be roughly equivalent to the present arrangements, not relying on funding benefits out of cuts in government expenditure elsewhere. After a decade in which many have almost given up hope of seeing significant improvements in health, it is elating to realise that a future Chancellor has it within his or her power to make substantial improvements even in a single widely acceptable budget.

---

* The tax-free status of pension fund income results in a very substantial loss of tax revenue — over £4 billion in 1987/88. If such tax benefits were reduced or eliminated it would seem that either higher contributions or lower pension payouts would result — but in fact pension funds have such large assets that this is not necessarily the case. It has been suggested that the losers would, in the long run, be the employers who are contributing on their employees' behalf. This is a technical matter that requires careful management not to disadvantage pension holders, but there seems no good reason why saving money through a pension scheme should have such tax advantages over other forms of saving.

**An alternative, less explored, avenue to redistributing wealth is to give wealth to the poor. This option, usually ignored by both left and right, has recently been explored by the advocates of 'market socialism' around the Fabian Society. They have suggested using the receipts of wealth taxes to provide a lump sum to everyone on reaching adulthood.[68]

Endnote

It is often suggested that just changing people's incomes is not enough to improve their health. While we acknowledge that there are numerous other ways of improving health, we would emphasise that the evidence does show that more equal income distribution is enough on its own to have a major impact on health. Indeed, evidence from the Health and Lifestyles Survey[69] suggests that poor people who adopt 'healthy' behaviour (good diet, exercise, not smoking) benefit their health less than the relatively well-off who adopt the same behaviour.

Nor do we want to suggest that it is not worth improving people's housing or other aspects of their material circumstances — indeed adding to income is in many cases one of the more effective ways of achieving such objectives. But because income distribution is much more important than absolute income, the implication is clearly that health is no longer determined primarily by the direct physical impact of our material circumstances. Instead, it seems to be a matter of how our circumstances compare with those of others — influencing our self-esteem, our ability to manage in an affluent world and our relations with others. Dealing directly with this inequality is the most effective way we know to improve health.

We have argued that improving the tax/benefit system presents the best opportunity for immediate and significant moves in this direction. This should therefore be the primary focus of activity within the public health field. But, in the longer term, the distribution of original incomes needs similar attention. For the vast majority of the population, access to stable employment in a reasonably-paid job offers the best security against poverty both during working life and retirement. Maximising the opportunities for such employment is an important part of any move towards greater equality — though it is worth remembering that it leaves the issue of supporting those in unpaid work to be addressed.

The creation of a society that can offer full employment of a suitable kind is a task that is only partly within the government's control. Macro-economic pressures often push government policies off-course. Increasingly international investment patterns, the impact on the West of changes in Eastern Europe, the apparent tendency of Western workers to polarise into a 'core' and a 'peripheral' workforce, suggest a changed economic order in which governments may find themselves with neither the knowledge nor the power to control their economies as they would wish. Demographic pressures are another major factor. The predicted increase in the dependency ratio seems likely to put workers in a stronger position than they have been for some years.*

This broader background will do much to determine the effectiveness of specific policies that may be implemented. One of the most crucial areas for action is low pay. This is a long standing problem. In 1982 the Department of Employment pointed out that the distribution of manual men's earnings had remained roughly constant for a century. The poorest workers were worse off, relative to the rest of the population, than they were in the 1880s.[70] In all, more than nine million workers, full and part-time — 44% of the adult workforce — earn below two-thirds of the median wage for the basic hours they work. Two out of three of these are women, and members of ethnic minorities are over-represented.[71] Low pay is increasing with Government policies to reduce employment rights, continuing unemployment and the fragmentation of the workforce.

One action within the Government's power is the introduction of a minimum wage. Britain is the only country in the EC without one, and the idea is increasingly widely accepted, though there is still concern from some quarters about the effect on employment levels.[71] The Labour Party is committed to the introduction of a minimum wage fixed at fifty percent of the adult average wage (pro rata for part-timers) moving to two-thirds of the median wage.[65] The payment of benefits to those also earning, such as Family Credit or social dividend proposals, adds to the case for a minimum wage. Without it, there is a risk that benefits could merely enable employers to offer lower wages in the knowledge that they would be topped up.

Reducing pay differentials across the spectrum is also of importance. The pattern of union wage claims and attitudes to differentials, as well as government pay policies, may have an effect. In addition, it would seem plausible that a high degree of hierarchical differentiation within the workplace would go hand in hand with increased income differentials. Japan has a comparatively egalitarian income distribution and restricted workplace hierarchies. Reducing hierarchy in the workplace might benefit income distribution and also, perhaps, have more direct benefits to workplace relations and self esteem.

Access to good quality employment is most limited for those in our society discriminated against in other ways — women, particularly when bringing up children, people with disabilities, carers and members of ethnic minorities. Many of the remedies are well-discussed — improved childcare, improved opportunity and protection for part-time workers, effective anti-discrimination legislation, quotas and good practice policies, increased training and education as well as an income support structure that makes working worth-while — these are just the beginning of the list. The Government also has considerable influence through regional policies to reduce the phenomenon of whole communities and regions of deprivation that come about from the knock-on effects of high unemployment. But although some of these policies — training, for example — may perhaps have an effect on the number of jobs available, in general it is hard to avoid the conclusion that the success of such strategies will be highly dependent on the overall economic and demographic trends influencing demand for labour. This re-emphasises the point that, important though original incomes are in the long term, in the short term aiming at redistribution through taxes and benefits is a safer strategy.

We said earlier that life is short where its quality is poor, and in many respects health is a good indicator of differences in the quality of life both within and between societies. Too often the material standard of living is regarded as synonymous with the quality of life and income is assumed to be its best measure. But indices of real income are unable to come to grips with the all-important qualitative changes in our way of life and are obliged to summarise all change as if it were a purely quantitative process. They cannot even take account of the qualitative changes in the material goods and services we consume. Health, on the other hand, is sensitive not only to both qualitative and quantitative changes in material life but also to its crucial psychological and social components. **Modern standards of consumption have reached a point where improving the distribution of what is produced is very much more important than further increasing its quantity. What is produced must be used more effectively to serve human goals.**

The reduction of income differentials and relative poverty are important enough objectives in terms of social justice alone. Their role as determinants of the population's health adds to its urgency. If these health effects are also indicative of the changes which need to be made in order to improve the quality of life and human happiness in society as a whole, they must not be ignored.

---

* OPCS population projections suggest that between 1985 and 20the number of children under 16 will increase by 8%, people aged 65 and over by 7% and 85 and over by 70% whereas the working population, defined as those aged 16-64, will increase by less than 2%.[49]

References

1   Preston, S, 1976, **Morality patterns in national populations**, Academic Press, London.

2   Rodgers, G B, 1979, Income and inequality as determinants of mortality: an international cross-section analysis, **Population Studies**, 33, 343-51.

3   Wilkinson, R G, 1986, Income and Mortality, in: **Class and Health: Research and Longitudinal Data** Edited by R G Wilkinson, Tavistock, London.

4   Wilkinson, R G, 1990, Income distribution and mortality: a natural experiment, **Sociology of Health and Illness** 12:4, 391-412.

5   Le Grand, J, 1987, **An international comparison of inequalities in health**, Welfare State Programme Discussion Paper No. 16, London School of Economics.

6   Wilkinson, R G, **Life Expectancy and Income Distribution,** British Medical Journal, 1991, forthcoming.

7   Marmot, M G and Davey Smith, G, 1989. Why are the Japanese living longer? **British Medical Journal**, 299, 1547-51.

8   DHSS, 1990, **On the state of the public health for the year 1989**, HMSO.

9   Winter, J M, 1988, Public health and the extension of life expectancy in England and Wales 1901-60, in: Keynes, M(ed), **The political economy of health and welfare**. Cambridge University Press, Cambridge.

10   Titmuss, R M, 1958, War and Social Policy, in: **Essays on the Welfare State**, p86, Unwin, London.

11   Wilkinson, R G, 1989, Class mortality differentials, income distribution and trends in poverty 1921-81, *Journal of Social Policy*, 18:3, 307-35.

12   Pamuk, E R, 1985, Social class inequality in mortality from 1921 to 1972 in England and Wales, *Population Studies*, 39, 17-31.

13   OPCS, 1978 *Occupational Mortality 1970-2*, Decennial Supplement, Series DS1.

14   Blaxter, M, 1990, *Health and Lifestyles, Tavistock, London.*

15   *Kehrer, B H and Wolin, C M, 1979, Impact of income maintenance on low birthweight, Journal of Human Resources*, XIV, 434-62.

16   Beale, N and Nethercott, S, 1988, The nature of unemployment morbidity, *Journal of the Royal College of General Practitioners*, 38, 200-2

17   Moser, K A, Goldblatt, P O and Fox, A J, 1987, Unemployment and Mortality 1981-3: follow-up of the 1981 Census sample, *British Medical Journal*, 294, 86-90.

18   Scott-Samuel, A, letter, *Lancet*, 1984, II, 1464-5

19   WHO, 1985, *Targets for health for all: targets in support of the European regional strategy for health for all*, WHO Regional Office for Europe, Copenhagen.

20   Wilkinson, R G, 1986, Socioeconomic differences in mortality: interpreting the data on their size and trends, in: *Class and Health*, op cit.

21   Power, C, Manor, O, Fox, A J and Fogelman, K, 1990, Health in childhood and social inequalities in health in young adults, *Journal of the Royal Statistical Society*, A, 153:1 17-28.

22   Pamuk, E R, 1988, Social class inequalities in infant mortality in England and Wales from 1921 to 1980, *European Journal of Populations*, 4, 1-21.

23   Marmot, M G, 1986, Social inequalities in mortality: the social environment, in: *Class and Health: research and longitudinal data*, Op cit

24   Rose, G and Marmot, M G, 1981, Social Class and CHD, *British Heart Journal*, 45, 13-19.

25   Rose, G, 1981, Strategy for prevention: lessons from cardiovascular disease, *British Medical Journal*, 282, 1847-51.

26   Gatherer, A, Parfit, J, Porter, E and Vessey, M, 1979, *Is health education effective?* Health Education Council, London.

27   Leon, D and Wilkinson, R G, 1989, Inequalities in prognosis: socioeconomic differences in cancer and heart disease survival, in A J Fox ed. loc cit.(29)

28   Hills, J, 1988, *Changing tax: how the tax system works and how to change it*, CPAG (1 p13, 2 p9, 3 p41)

29   Fox, A J, (ed), 1989, *Health inequalities in European Countries*, Gower, Aldershot.

30   Martin, C J, Platt, S D and Hunt, S M, 1987, Housing conditions and ill health, *British Medical Journal*, 294, 1125-7.

31   Townsend, P, 1979, *Poverty in the United Kingdom*, Penguin, Harmondsworth.

32   Burghes, L, 1980, *Living from hand to mouth: a study of 65 families living on supplementary benefit*, Child Poverty Action Group/Family Service Unit.

33   Lang, T, Andrews, C, Bedale, C, Hannon, E and Hulme, J, 1984, *Jam Tomorrow*, Food Policy Unit, Hollings Faculty, University of Manchester.

34   DHSS, 1979, *Nutrition and Health in old age*, Reports on Health and Social Subjects No. 16, HMSO.

35   Conway, J et al, 1988, *Prescription for Poor Health: the crisis for homeless families*, London Food Commission, Maternity Alliance, SHAC, Shelter.

36   Greve, J and Currie, E, 1990, *Homelessness in Britain*, Joseph Rowntree Memorial Trust.

37   Palmore, E, 1969, Predicting longevity, *Gerontologist*, 9, 247.

38   OPCS, 1984, *General Household Survey, GHS 1982*, HMSO.

39   Cook, D G, Cummings, R O, Bartley, M J and Shaper, A G, 1982, Health of unemployed middle-aged men in Great Britain, *Lancet*, I, 1290-4.

40   Yates, F et al, 1984, *Drinking in Two North-East Towns*, Newcastle Centre for Alcohol and Drug Studies.

41   Fazey, C, Brown, P and Batey, P, 1990, *A socio-demographic analysis of patients attending a drug dependency clinic*, Studies of Drug Issues, Report No. 5, Centre for Urban Studies, University of Liverpool.

42   Berkman, L, 1984, Assessing the physical health effects of social networks and social support, *American Journal of Public Health*, 5, 413-32.

43   Cohen, S and Syme, S L (eds.), 1985, *Social Support and Health*, Academic Press, London.

44   Brown, G and Harris, T, 1978, *The Social Origins of Depression*, Tavistock London.

45   Siegrist, L and Halhuber, M J, 1981, *Myocardial infarction and psychosocial risks*, Springer-Verlag, Berlin.

46   Golding, P (ed), 1986, *Excluding the Poor*, Child Poverty Action Group, 1-5 Bath Street, London EC1V 9PY.

47   Mack, J and Lansley, S, 1985, *Poor Britain*, Allen and Unwin.

48   Smeeding, T H, O'Higgins, M, and Rainwater, L (eds), 1990, *Poverty, Inequality and Income Distribution in Comparative Perspective: The Luxembourg Income Study*, Wheatsheaf.

49   Parker, H, 1989, *Instead of the Dole: An enquiry into integration of the tax and benefit system*, Routledge. (1 p303, 2 p73, 3 p16, 4 p71, 5 p297).

50   Lansley, S and Mack, J, 1983, *Breadline Britain*, London Weekend Television.

51   Frayman, H, 1991, *Breadline Britain 1990s*, London Weekend Television.

52   Lipsy, D, 1986, New Society, 18 April.

53   Jowell, R et al (eds), 1988, *British Social Attitudes 1987*, 5th Report, Social and Community Planning Research, Gower.

54   Oppenheim, C, 1990, *Poverty: the facts*, Child Poverty Action Group, 1-5 Bath Street, London EC1V 9PY.

55   Jowell, R et al (eds), 1990, *British Social Attitudes, Special International Report, 6th Report*, Social and Community Planning Research, Gower.

56   Central Statistical Office, 1990, *Family Expenditure Survey 1989*, HMSO.

57   Pahl, J, 1983, *The Allocation of Money and the Structuring of Inequality within Marriage*, Sociological Review 31, 237-262.

58   Atkinson, A B, 1985, *Income Maintenance and Social Insurance: A survey*, Discussion paper 5, Welfare State Programme, London School of Economics.

59   Piachaud, D, 1990, *Poverty and Social Security*, mimeograph, London School of Economics.

60   Lister, R, 1987, *There is an Alternative: Reforming Social Security*, Child Poverty Action Group.

61   Le Grand, J and Winter, D, 1987, *The Middle Classes and the Welfare State*, Discussion paper 14, Welfare State Programme, London School of Economics.

62   Bidwell, S, Potter, T and Rice, C, 1990, *The Growing Divide: Poverty, Health and Government Reform of the National Health Service*, West Midlands Low Pay Unit and West Midlands Health Service Monitoring Unit.

63   National Consumer Council, 1984, *Of Benefit to All*, NCC.

64   Esam, P, Good, R and Middleton, R, 1985, *Who's to Benefit? A Radical Review of the Social Security System*, Verso.

65   The Labour Party, 1991, *Labour: Opportunity Britain*.

66   Vince, P, 1986, *Basic Incomes: Some Practical Considerations*, BIRG Bulletin 5, Basic Income Research Group, 102 Pepys Road, London SE14 5SG.

67   Central Statistical Office, 1991, *Social Trends 1991*, HMSO.

68   Le Grand, J, 1989, Markets, Welfare and Equality, in Le Grand, J and Estrin, S, 1989, *Market Socialism*, Clarendon Press, 193-292.

69   Blaxter, M, 1990, *Health and Lifestyle*, Tavistock.

70   Department of Employment, 1982, *Employment Gazette*, HMSO.

71   Low Pay Forum, 1988, *Britain can't afford low pay: A programme for a national minimum wage*, Low Pay Unit, 9 Upper Berkeley St, London W1H 8BY.